PURE & SIMPLE

HOMEMADE INDIAN VEGETARIAN CUISINE

ISBN: 978-81-7436-592-7

© Text & images: Vidhu Mittal
vidhu.mittal@gmail.com

© Roli Books Pvt. Ltd., 2014
Fifth impression
Published in India by Roli Books
M-75, Greater Kailash II Market
New Delhi-110 048, India
Phone: ++91-11-40682000
Fax: ++91-1129217185
Email: info@rolibooks.com
Website: www.rolibooks.com

Editor: Neeta Datta
Design: Supriya Saran
Production: Naresh Nigam

Printed and bound in India

PURE & SIMPLE

HOMEMADE INDIAN VEGETARIAN CUISINE

VIDHU MITTAL

Photographs
SANJAY RAMCHANDRAN

Lustre Press
Roli Books

For every vegetarian food lover

ACKNOWLEDGEMENTS

Sanjay Ramchandran who very patiently took photographs. His creativity reflects in this book.

Jagdish Babu DK who systematically rearranged selected photographs and text. It was a boon for a non-tech savvy person like me to have him around.

Sujatha Puranik Rakhra, an invaluable sounding board, who was always there for me whenever I needed her.

Abhishek Poddar, who has a creative eye, gave several ideas for the layout and the cover page.

William GK who assisted in the final styling of each dish before it was shot.

And, most importantly, my husband, **Som**, our children, **Nidhi, Tarang** and **Siddharth**, my sister, **Anu**, and my domestic help, **Madamma**, who supported me as I journeyed through this book.

CONTENTS

FOREWORD

Even before our father's job took us to Bangalore, our parents were great hosts. They loved having friends and family over for vivacious gatherings. Aside from the great company, the hallmark of these events was, undeniably, food.

The spreads were highlighted with Indian classics like *dal makhani* and *methi paneer,* as well as continental gems like corn with spinach, casseroles, and potato with mixed vegetable cakes.

As our parents' social circle grew larger and more eclectic, so did the opportunity for the two of them to hone their entertaining skills.

It was during this time that a close friend of our mother's, and a regular at these gatherings, encouraged her to consider sharing her culinary skills. Our family jumped onboard, making posters for 'Fancy Chef Cookery Classes'.

Her first course – Party Cooking – spanned five days, during the work week, and had two simple tenets: vegetarianism and delighting a crowd. For three hours, every day, our dining room was transformed into a working kitchen, complete with a portable stove, notebooks, and raw ingredients. Five housewives made up the first class. Her tasty, yet easy-to-prepare recipes, along with her straightforward teaching style lead to all five returning for the sequel: Party Cooking 2.

With these humble beginnings, in culinary pedagogy, Mom expanded her selection of classes to include international cuisine. When dining at the newest eatery in Bangalore, she always tried to figure out, how to recreate the dishes. And then we'd return home to be guinea pigs for her experiments.

Nobody ever heard the two of us complain. For sixteen years, we have watched her make many aspiring cooks (and as a consequence, their families) very happy. This book is a culmination of what she's learned and is sure to spread that joy to many more.

Nidhi and Tarang

INTRODUCTION

Around the globe, popularity in both Indian cuisine and vegetarianism is rising steadily. This book will introduce you to the joys of cooking and even show how it can actually be a relaxing activity. Arming you with simple methods, this book will allow you to recreate the intricate flavours, intoxicating aromas, and succulent textures of homely Indian food.

I have been conducting cookery classes in Bangalore, India, for over 15 years and it has been one of my most rewarding experiences. My many students have been the source of encouragement and inspiration for writing this book.

The recipes in this book have the characteristic flavour of my native province – Uttar Pradesh. My emphasis has been on crafting delicately spiced dishes, contrary to the hot flavours stereotypically associated with Indian cuisine.

Combinations of these recipes make for delicious menus that are also very well-balanced meals. You will find many ways to pick and choose various courses like soups, salads, refreshing drinks, entrées, and scrumptious desserts.

I have had the opportunity to perfect these recipes over the years. With these dishes, I have also tried to illustrate the immense visual appeal of Indian food and highlight the natural colours of the freshest ingredients. The preparations for these recipes involve very simple and easy-to-understand steps. Photographs accompany all the recipes and highlight each step of the process.

I hope you and your loved ones enjoy cooking these dishes as much as I have enjoyed writing this book.

Vidhu Mittal

DISCOVER SPICES

Spices are essential food additives enhancing flavour, aroma, and also colour to the food. These are natural and dried and used either whole or in powdered form. Some of these can be sprinkled but the true flavours get enhanced when roasted or preheated in cooking medium or when added during cooking. Spices must be stored in airtight containers to retain freshness.

Asafoetida (*hing*): It is a resin from a tree and has a strong smell when raw, but when cooked it imparts a smooth flavour. This spice aides in digestion and is used in food as a condiment. It must be stored away from other spices because of its strong odour.

Bay leaf (*tej patta*): It is a dry leaf of bay laurel tree, which has a pleasant flavour. Normally a dish is seasoned with 2-3 leaves. The fragrance of bay leaf is more obvious than the taste in cooked food. Leaves can be removed before serving.

Black cardamom (*badi elaichi*): It is a hairy brown pod which is used whole or crushed to add flavour to a dish. Black cardamom can be used in soups, rice, and savoury dishes and is discarded while eating. It is also used in the preparation of the Indian spice mixture called *garam* masala.

Black peppercorn (*sabut kali mirch*): It is a sun-dried berry of a pepper plant. Black peppercorn is sometimes used whole or in powdered form. It is also the main ingredient in the Indian spice mixture called *garam* masala.

Black salt (*kala namak*): It is an unrefined mineral salt, greyish in colour. It is used extensively in Indian cooking as it enhances the flavour in *chaats* and savouries.

Carom (*ajwain*) **seeds**: Carom seeds are greyish brown in colour; they are aromatic and slightly pungent in taste. Only a small quantity added to clarified butter (*ghee*) or oil is enough to flavour the dish. This helps reduce flatulence.

Chilli powder (*lal mirch*): It is a hot spice prepared from ground red chillies and the spiciness varies with the type of chilli used. Small quantity of chilli powder is added to oil while cooking curries. It can also be sprinkled over *chaat* and *raita* to add an extra zing. Kashmiri red chillies are often used as they add colour and are less spicy.

Cinnamon (*dalchini*): This is a bark of a tree, at times rolled and then dried. Cinnamon has an aromatic and sweet flavour. Powdered cinnamon is widely used in soups, desserts, and stews. Cinnamon sticks are used for indirect flavouring in a dish and may be removed while eating.

Clove (*laung*): It is an aromatic dried flower bud. It is used for both sweet and savoury dishes. Rice and soups seasoned with cloves in ghee or oil infuse a soothing flavour.

Coriander (*dhaniya*) **seeds**: These are dried fruits of the coriander / cilantro plant, greenish brown in colour with a slight savoury flavour. Powdered coriander is widely used in Indian curries.

Cumin (*jeera*) **seeds**: These are small, elongated seeds which have a distinctive aroma and flavour. Cumin seeds emit their own flavour after browning in oil for curries. They can also be roasted and ground and are used for flavouring yoghurt dishes.

Fennel (*saunf*) **seeds**: These are small, elongated, aromatic flavoured, and light green in colour. They have a sweet taste. Powdered fennel seeds are used in curries and pickles. Whole seeds are often chewed in India as a mouth freshener.

Fenugreek seeds (*methi dana*): These are hard and pale yellow in colour with a bitter taste. Only a few seeds are added for seasoning and flavouring. Powdered or whole seeds used in Indian pickles leave a pleasant aroma.

Green cardamom (*choti elaichi*): These are light green in colour with tiny, black seeds inside. The cardamom seeds are powdered and used in sweet dishes, tea, and some exotic dishes. Green cardamom has a distinctive refreshing flavour and is also a good mouth freshener.

 Jaggery (*gur*): This is boiled and solidified raw sugarcane juice, used extensively in Indian cooking. It has a unique flavour and is used in sweets and savoury dishes. It is considered healthier than sugar as it retains more mineral salts.

 Mango powder (*amchur*): This is the sun-dried powdered form of raw mangoes. It is generally added to the cooked vegetables towards the end to give a tangy flavour to the dish. Adding earlier can delay the cooking process.

 Mint (*pudina*) **powder**: This is the sun-dried powdered form of the fragrant aromatic plant of mint. It is used for adding a refreshing flavour to drinks, dry vegetables, Indian breads, and curries. Mint powder can be stored for up to a month.

 Mustard seeds (*rai*): These are small, round seeds from the mustard plant. The colour varies from black, brown to yellow. Savoury dishes are tempered with mustard seeds, and powdered mustard is used in pickles to give a sour taste. Bottled mustard paste is used for salad dressing and accompaniments.

 Nutmeg (*jaiphal*): It is oval with a spicy flavour and aroma and is always used grated. It is used to flavour vegetables, soups, cakes, and puddings.

 Saffron (*kesar*): Saffron strands are dried stigmas of the saffron crocus flower. It is an expensive and exotic spice. Saffron strands are generally infused in hot water or hot milk to extract its colour and delicate flavour.

 Sesame (*til*) **seeds**: These are generally found in two colours: white and brown. It has a nutty taste and emits more flavour when roasted. Roasted seeds are ground and mixed to prepare desserts and savoury dishes.

 Turmeric (*haldi*) **powder**: It is an underground stem which resembles fresh ginger. It is bright yellow in colour. Powdered turmeric is an important ingredient in Indian curries and has an earthy, bitter flavour. It also acts as an anti-bacterial agent.

KNOW YOUR VEGETABLES

LEAFY GREENS

Spinach (*palak*): Spinach has dark green, smooth leaves and is generally cooked, but the young leaves are often used in salads. It has a bitter-sweet flavour. The most common way to prepare spinach is by sautéing with other vegetables or lentils.

Spring onion (*hara pyaz*): Also known as salad onion, this vegetable normally has small white bulbs at the tip and is ideal for stir-fry dishes. Spring onion has a mild flavour and is, therefore, relished in salads.

Mint (*pudina*): The leaves have a fresh aromatic, sweet flavour with a menthol after taste. Mint leaves are also used in beverages and ice creams.

Fenugreek (*methi*): Fenugreek leaves have a strong, bitter flavour with a characteristic aroma.

Curry leaves (*kadhi patta*): Curry leaves come from the curry tree, a short tree whose leaves resemble those of the neem plant. The leaves are commonly used for seasoning. They can also be used in the dried form, but fresh leaves have a superior aroma.

Coriander / Cilantro (*dhaniya*): All parts of this leafy plant are edible. Heat diminishes the flavour of coriander leaves very quickly and hence they are most commonly used in the final step of preparing a dish, typically as a garnish. The leaves are best stored, refrigerated, in airtight containers.

Lemon grass: Lemon grass has a strong lemon-like flavour and is the main ingredient in Thai cuisine. The stems of fresh lemon grass are tough. The chopped grass can be bruised to release its flavour, if used whole in cooking then remove before serving.

GREEN VEGETABLES

Zucchini: Zucchini is a variety of squash, with shiny, edible outer skin. The flesh is white inside with a delicate flavour. Yellow zucchini is also available.

Raw mango (*kairi*): It is a large tropical fruit found in many varieties; raw mango is oblong and greenish. It is primarily used for making pickles and chutneys.

Okra (*bhindi*): Also known as lady's finger, okra is fairly popular in Indian cuisine. It looks like a capsule about 6-12 cm long. Its big white seeds are tender when cooked and contribute a lot to the flavour of the vegetable.

Green peas (*hara mattar*): Also known as garden peas, fresh peas are bright green pods. The peas inside are glossy, crunchy, and sweet. Shell just before using. Green peas are a fair source of vitamins A and C and iron.

Green chilli: The most commonly used vegetable in Indian cooking is the small green chilli. A good substitute for this could be the Thai green chilli. It has a very sharp and pungent spiciness, and is frequently used to flavour a dish right from the start.

Green banana (*kacha kela*): Green banana or raw banana is used in many parts of India. It is hard and crunchy when raw. Raw banana softens when heated or pressure cooked and has a fibrous texture.

Green beans: These are mostly fat and fleshy, and firm when fresh. Steamed and sautéed, beans can also be used in salads. Green beans contain a fair amount of vitamins A and C.

Broccoli: Broccoli belongs to the cabbage family, and has fleshy, dark green flower heads. It is quick and easy to prepare, and can be eaten boiled or steamed or raw with a dip of your choice. Broccoli is also used in soups and side dishes.

Bell pepper (*Shimla mirch*): Bell pepper and chillies are members of the capsicum family. Green bell pepper has a fresh raw flavour, whereas the red, yellow and orange ones are sweeter. Pepper can be fried with onion and garlic, braised with tomatoes, combined with potatoes, and used raw in salads.

ROOT VEGETABLES

Potato: Potato is a starchy, tuberous root vegetable. It is an important source of carbohydrate. It also contains potassium, iron, and vitamins B and C. Potato can be boiled, baked, deep-fried, sautéed, mashed or roasted.

Sweet potato (*shakarkandi*): Sweet potato is a starchy and sweet-tasting root vegetable. The skin colour ranges from white to pink to reddish brown. Sweet potato can be baked or boiled and has a distinct sweet and savoury flavour. It is used in savoury and salad dishes.

Carrot (*gajar*): Carrot is a root vegetable, either orange or red in colour, with a crisp texture when fresh. It has a sweet and fragrant flavour when eaten raw. Carrot can be cooked in many ways. Carrot juice is a healthy drink and can also be blended with salad dressing. It is rich in carotene and vitamin A.

Colocasia (*arvi*): Colocasia is a round or elongated tuberous, hairy root vegetable. It is boiled like potato, peeled, and then used. It has a sticky flesh.

Ginger (*adrak*): Fresh ginger is pale in colour with knobbly roots. Ginger flavour is peppery and slightly sweet, while the aroma is pungent and spicy. Ginger has the quality of enhancing and complementing both sweet and savoury food. It is used to spice cookies, cakes, tea, coffee, jams, and pickles.

Radish (*mooli*): Radish can be found in multiple varieties. The one most commonly used in Indian cooking is in the Daikon family. It has long, white, elongated and smooth roots. The raw flesh of these roots has a crisp and crunchy texture. The taste is pungent and sharp – almost peppery.

GOURDS

Bitter gourd (*karela*): Also known as bitter melon, this is a fruit with a warty texture on the outside. The flesh part is thin and the entire fruit is pretty hollow with large seeds. It is best cooked when it is green and not ripened. This vegetable has a strong bitter flavour. Salting, followed by washing, can mitigate the bitterness a little.

Bottle gourd (*lauki*)
Also known as calabash, bottle gourd is large and hollow. The freshest samples have a light green skin and white flesh. It is cooked most often like a squash. It can be the main ingredient in a lot of recipes but also compliments other dishes like lentils very well.

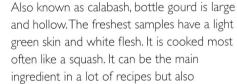

Ridge gourd (*turai*): Ridge gourd has even ridges running down the exterior at regular intervals. It is typically harvested before maturity. At that stage it is light green in colour and has tender flesh.

Cucumber (*khira*): Cucumber is a long, green, cylindrical fruit of the gourd family with edible seeds and crisp flesh. It is normally eaten raw in salads. The young cucumber is used for making pickles.

MISCELLANEOUS VEGETABLES

Cauliflower (*phool gobi*): While cauliflower is available in many colours, the most popular among these is the white variety. It can be prepared in a number of ways like boiled, roasted, fried, steamed or even eaten raw. It is low in fat and high in dietary fiber and vitamin C.

Cabbage (*bandh gobi*): Cabbage is widely used in Indian cooking. The part of the plant normally consumed is the immature bunch of leaves that are light green in colour. It is most often prepared by sautéing and also compliments other vegetables like peas and potatoes.

Onion (*pyaz*): Onion is an integral part of Indian cuisine adding a delicate aroma when cooked and a sharp taste when added raw as a garnish.

Baby onion / Pearl onion: Baby onion is most commonly used in stews. However, it can just easily be used in saucy and dry dishes alike. The flavour is sweeter than normal onions.

Garlic (*lasan*): Garlic is widely used for its pungent flavour. It is typically paired with ginger for a richer, aromatic taste. It has a very long shelf life and is typically stored in warm dry conditions.

Tomato: Tomato found in India is very similar to the Italian Roma tomato. It is widely used in Indian cooking, especially as a base for many sauces. It is also very popularly consumed in its raw form.

Cherry tomato: Cherry tomato is the smaller variety of the traditional tomato. It is a little sweeter in taste and is most commonly consumed raw in salads.

Lemon (*nimbu*): Freshly squeezed lemon juice adds great flavour to most foods. The acidity it provides can really enrich the taste of an otherwise bland dish.

Pumpkin (*kaddu, kaashiphal*): Pumpkin, found in India, is typically dark orange and sometimes almost red. It tends to have a thick flesh but is otherwise mostly hollow containing a mesh of seeds. The seeds aren't typically used in cooking while the flesh is consumed widely.

Baby corn (*bhutta*): Baby corn is harvested premature corn, which is typically 5-10 cm long. It is consumed whole along with the cob. It is tender and provides a nice crunchiness to the dish to which they are added.

GOODNESS OF LENTILS

The edible seeds of peas and beans are known as lentils and are also considered as pulses. Highly nutritious, lentils can be used in soups, curries or as an accompanying vegetable. A variety of lentils exist with colours that range from yellow to red-orange to green, brown and black. Lentils are sold in many forms, with or without the skins, whole or split. They contain high levels of proteins, vitamin B1, dietary fiber, and minerals.

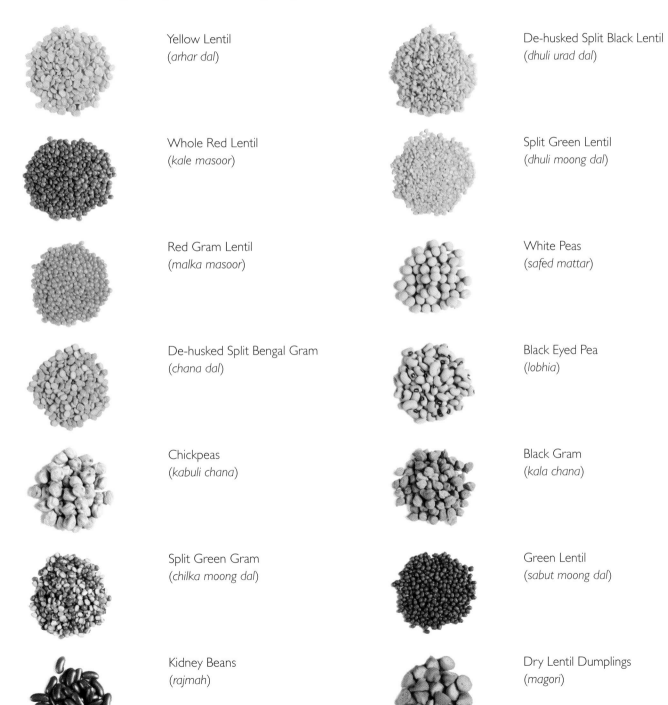

Yellow Lentil
(*arhar dal*)

Whole Red Lentil
(*kale masoor*)

Red Gram Lentil
(*malka masoor*)

De-husked Split Bengal Gram
(*chana dal*)

Chickpeas
(*kabuli chana*)

Split Green Gram
(*chilka moong dal*)

Kidney Beans
(*rajmah*)

De-husked Split Black Lentil
(*dhuli urad dal*)

Split Green Lentil
(*dhuli moong dal*)

White Peas
(*safed mattar*)

Black Eyed Pea
(*lobhia*)

Black Gram
(*kala chana*)

Green Lentil
(*sabut moong dal*)

Dry Lentil Dumplings
(*magori*)

KITCHEN EQUIPMENT

Pressure cooker

Skillet

Grater (*kaddu kas*)

Griddle (*tawa*)

Deep-frying wok (*kadhai*)

Deep strainer

Saucepan

Measuring cup

Idli stand

Colander (*chalni*)

Spice box (*masala dani*)

Tongs (*chimta*)

Strainer (*chai ki chalni*)

Sieve / Sifter (*chhanni*)

Tempering ladle
(*chouk ki kalchi*)

Rolling board and rolling pin
(*chakla-belan*)

Chopping board

Pestle and motar (*moosal*)

Potato masher

Wire whisk

Vegetable peeler

Melon scoop

Knives (*churi / chaku*)

Pancake turner (*palta*)

Spatula (*jharni*)

Ladle (*kalchi*)

Boondi ladle

DRINKS, SOUPS & SALADS

SPICED YOGHURT DRINK
Mattha

INGREDIENTS

1 cup / 200 gm Yoghurt (*dahi*)
½ tsp / 2½ gm Roasted cumin (*jeera*) powder (see p. 184)
Salt to taste
¼ tsp Mint (*pudina*) powder (see p. 11)
¼ tsp Black salt (*kala namak*)
2 cups / 400 ml Water
Coriander (*dhaniya*) leaves, chopped for garnishing

METHOD

- Whisk the yoghurt. Add roasted cumin powder, salt to taste, mint powder, and black salt. Stir to mix well.

- Add water and mix well.

- Serve chilled garnished with coriander leaves.

- Spiced yoghurt drink gives a cool refreshing feeling during summer.

ICED TEA
Sharbati Chai

INGREDIENTS

For the tea syrup:
1¼ cups / 250 gm Sugar
1 cup / 200 ml Water
6 tbsp Lemon grass, chopped
5 tsp / 25 gm Tea leaves
2 tbsp / 30 ml Lemon (*nimbu*) juice

For each serving:
2 tbsp / 30 ml Prepared tea syrup
2 tsp / 10 ml Lemon juice
2 tsp / 10 ml Honey
Ice cubes
2 Lemon, slices
8 Mint (*pudina*) leaves
½ cup / 100 ml Chilled water

METHOD

• **For the tea syrup**, mix sugar, water, and lemon grass in a pan. Boil on low heat till the sugar dissolves. Add tea leaves and turn off the heat. Leave covered for 20 minutes.

• Strain the tea mixture, cool and add 2 tbsp lemon juice. Keep aside.

• In each serving glass, put 2 tbsp tea syrup, 2 tsp lemon juice, 2 tsp honey, and fill with ice cubes.

• Add lemon slices and mint leaves. Fill with chilled water and serve.

• Iced tea is an unusually flavoured substitute for aerated drinks.

MANGO MOCKTAIL
Aam Panna

Serves: 4-6

INGREDIENTS

2 / 250 gm Raw mangoes (*kairi*), medium-sized, pressure cooked, peeled, pulp removed (see p. 183)
Salt to taste
4 tbsp Mint (*pudina*) leaves
2 tbsp / 30 gm Sugar, powdered
1 tsp / 5 gm Roasted cumin (*jeera*) powder (see p. 184)

For each serving:
Gram flour granules (*boondi*-see p. 168), crushed ice and mint sprigs

METHOD

• Blend the mango pulp with 4 cups water, salt to taste, and mint leaves.

• Strain the mixture in a sieve.

• Add sugar and roasted cumin powder to the mango mixture; mix well and chill.

• Add crushed ice in each glass pour the drink, and serve garnished with 2 tsp gram flour granules and mint sprigs.

• Two mangoes will give approximately 1½ cups of pulp.
• Mango mocktail is a good summer drink as it prevents heat stroke.

• Gram flour granule (*boondi*) packets are available in any Indian grocery store.

ORANGE GLORY
Narangi Savera

INGREDIENTS
3-4 Oranges (*santara*), peeled, broken into segments, chilled
125 gm Papaya (*papita*), cut into medium-sized cubes, chilled
2 tbsp / 30 gm Sugar, powdered
¼ tsp Black salt (*kala namak*)
1½ cups / 300 ml Water
1 tsp / 5 ml Lemon (*nimbu*) juice
Crushed ice for serving

METHOD
• Blend the chilled oranges and cut papaya with sugar, black salt, and water in a mixer.

• Strain and add lemon juice.

• Add crushed ice to individual glasses, pour the fruit mixture and serve.

• Red papaya tastes better in this drink.

• This is a delightful and healthy breakfast drink.

TENDER COCONUT COOLER
Daab Shikanji

INGREDIENTS

2 cups / 400 ml Tender coconut water (*daab*), chilled
400 ml Lemon soda, chilled
½ tsp / 2½ gm Black salt (*kala namak*)
2 tsp / 10 ml Honey

For the garnishing:

1 tbsp / 15 gm Tender coconut flesh (*malai*), chopped
1 tsp Coriander (*dhaniya*) leaves, chopped
250 gm Papaya (*papita*)

METHOD

- Scoop out 8 papaya spheres with a fruit scooper and keep aside.

- Mix coconut water, lemon soda, black salt, and honey together.

- Pour into individual glasses. Serve garnished with chopped tender coconut flesh, coriander leaves, and papaya spheres.

- Tender coconut water is rich in mineral salts.
- It acts as a coolant for the digestive system.

- The flesh of the tender coconut has a soft creamy texture and can be easily scooped out and chopped.

MINTY LEMONADE
Hara Bhara Nimbu Pani

INGREDIENTS

1 tbsp / 15 ml Lemon (*nimbu*) juice
1½ tbsp / 25 gm Sugar
¼ tsp Black salt (*kala namak*)
4-6 Mint (*pudina*) leaves
¾ cup / 150 ml Water
Ice for serving

METHOD

• Put lemon juice, sugar, black salt, mint, and water into a mixer jar and blend well.

• Pour into a tall serving glass.

• Serve with ice.

• Minty lemonade is a healthy substitute for carbonated drinks.

• Calorie watchers can use sugar substitutes.

TOMATO CUCUMBER MELODY
Tamatar Khira Lajawab

Serves: 4

INGREDIENTS

4 / 400 gm Red tomatoes,
medium-sized, cut into 8 pieces
2 cups / 400 ml Water
Salt to taste
¼ tsp Black pepper (*kali mirch*)
2 tsp / 10 gm Sugar, powdered
For serving: mix together
2 tbsp / 30 gm Cucumber
(*khira*), finely chopped
1 tbsp / 15 gm Capsicum
(*Shimla mirch*), finely chopped
½ tbsp Mint (*pudina*), chopped
½ tbsp Coriander (*dhaniya*)
leaves, chopped

METHOD

• Heat 5 cups water for 4
minutes, turn off the heat.
Add the cut tomatoes and
leave them covered for half
an hour. Remove and chill the
tomatoes.

• Blend the chilled tomatoes
in a mixer with 2 cups water
and strain.

• Add salt, black pepper, and
sugar. Mix and chill.

• **For serving**, put 1 tbsp
chopped vegetable mixture
into individual glasses, fill with
tomato juice and serve.

• Do not liquidize the tomatoes without blanching, to ensure that the
pulp and liquid do not separate.

• Tomato cucumber melody makes a healthy, refreshing lunch-time

CARROT SOUP
Gajar Shorba

Serves: 4

INGREDIENTS

4 / 200 gm Carrots (*gajar*),
medium-sized, cut into cubes
1 / 75 gm Potato, medium-sized,
cut into cubes
2 tsp / 10 gm Butter
2 tsp / 10 gm Coriander
(*dhaniya*) leaf paste
Salt to taste
6 Black peppercorns (*sabut kali
mirch*), crushed
½ tsp / 2½ gm Sugar

METHOD

• Heat 1 tsp butter in a
pressure cooker for 30
seconds; add carrots and
potato and cook for a
minute. Add 3½ cups water
and pressure cook till one
whistle. Cool, blend and
strain. Keep aside.

• Grind the coriander leaves in
a mortar to a fine paste.

• Heat 1 tsp butter in a pan;
add coriander leaf paste and
sauté for 10 seconds. Add the
strained vegetable mixture,
salt, black pepper, and sugar;
bring to the boil, and simmer
for 2 minutes. Serve hot.

• Carrot soup is a quick healthy soup which can be prepared with red
or orange carrots.

• This soup can be garnished with cream or freshly ground pepper,
if desired.

GREEN PEA SOUP
Mattar Shorba

Serves: 4-6

INGREDIENTS

For the soup stock:

2 cups / 200 gm Green peas (*hara mattar*), shelled

2 cups / 100 gm Spinach (*palak*), chopped

1 tbsp Mint (*pudina*), chopped

Other Ingredients

2 tsp / 10 gm Butter

1 cup / 200 ml Milk

Salt and black pepper (*kali mirch*) to taste

¼ tsp Sugar

¼ tsp Nutmeg (*jaiphal*) powder

2 tsp / 10 ml Lemon (*nimbu*) juice

Fried bread croutons for garnishing

METHOD

• **For the soup stock**, melt 1 tsp butter in a pressure cooker; add green peas, spinach, and mint; cook for 30 seconds. Add 2½ cups water and pressure cook till one whistle. Simmer for 2 minutes.

• Remove, cool, blend and strain.

• Melt 1 tsp butter in a pan; add strained soup stock, milk, salt, black pepper to taste, sugar, and nutmeg powder. Bring to the boil, simmer for 2 minutes and then remove from heat.

• Add lemon juice and fried bread croutons just before serving.

• Mint adds a unique flavour to the soup.
• To retain the green colour of the soup, remove the lid from the pressure cooker after the pressure drops and cover the soup with a wire mesh.

SPINACH SOUP
Palak Shorba

Serves: 4

INGREDIENTS

400 gm Spinach (*palak*),
chopped, washed
½ tsp / 2½ gm Sugar
1 tsp / 5 gm Butter
1 cup / 200 ml Milk
Salt and black pepper (*kali mirch*) to taste
¼ tsp Nutmeg (*jaiphal*) powder
Cream for garnishing

METHOD

• Boil 5 cups water; add spinach and ¼ tsp sugar; cook for 4 minutes and drain. Cool and blend with 2½ cups water.

• Melt 1 tsp butter in a pan; add blended spinach, milk, salt, black pepper to taste, nutmeg powder, and ¼ tsp sugar.

• Bring the mixture to the boil, simmer for 2 minutes and remove from heat.

• Serve hot garnished with cream.

• Spinach soup is enriched with iron and is very good for growing children.

• The calorie conscious can omit the cream.

TOMATO SOUP
Tamatar Shorba

INGREDIENTS

6 / 600 gm Tomatoes, ripe, cut into 8 pieces
2 / 100 gm Carrots (*gajar*), medium-sized, cut into cubes
1 tsp / 5 gm Butter
Salt to taste
½ tsp / 2½ gm Sugar
1 tsp / 5 gm Roasted cumin (*jeera*) powder (see p. 184)
¼ tsp Black peppercorns (*sabut kali mirch*), freshly ground

For the garnishing:
1 cup Fried bread croutons
Coriander (*dhaniya*) leaves, chopped
Cream

METHOD

• Pressure cook the tomatoes and carrots with 2 cups water till one whistle.

• Keep aside to cool. Blend in a mixer and strain.

• Melt 1 tsp butter in a pan; add strained tomato mixture, salt to taste, sugar, roasted cumin powder, and black pepper powder. Bring to the boil and simmer for 5 minutes.

• Serve hot garnished with fried bread croutons, coriander leaves, and cream.

• Tomato soup is a popular and an all-time favourite soup.
• Carrots give this soup its body and additional flavour.

• Bread croutons are ½" cubes, deep-fried or sautéed till crisp.

VEGETABLE GARDEN SOUP
Sabz Baghan Shorba

Serves: 4-6

INGREDIENTS

2 tbsp / 30 gm Green Gram (*dhuli moong dal*), washed, soaked for 30 minutes
2 / 200 gm Tomatoes, large, cut into 8 pieces
1 / 50 gm Carrot (*gajar*), medium-sized, cut into cubes
1 tsp / 5 gm Butter
½ cup / 50 gm Carrots, grated
½ cup / 50 gm Cabbage (*bandh gobi*), shredded
½ cup / 50 gm Tomatoes, chopped
Salt and black pepper (*kali mirch*) to taste
¼ tsp Sugar
2 tsp / 10 ml Lemon (*nimbu*) juice
½ cup / 25 gm Spinach (*palak*), finely chopped

METHOD

• Pressure cook the soaked green gram, tomatoes, and carrot with 3 cups water till one whistle. Cool, blend and strain.

• Melt 1 tsp butter in a pan; add grated carrots, shredded cabbage, and chopped tomatoes; sauté for 30 seconds. Add the strained tomato mixture, salt, black pepper to taste, and sugar.

• Bring the mixture to the boil and simmer for 5 minutes. Remove from heat.

• Add lemon juice and chopped spinach, mix and serve hot.

• This soup can be garnished with fried bread croutons.

• This is a healthy soup with a combination of lentil and vegetables.

CHICKPEA SOUP
Kabuli Chana Shorba

INGREDIENTS

1 cup / 175 gm Chickpeas (*kabuli chana*), boiled (see p. 193)
1 cup / 150 gm Potatoes, chopped
2 tsp / 10 gm Butter
¼ cup / 50 gm Onion, chopped
½ tsp / 2½ gm Cumin (*jeera*) powder
½ tsp / 2½ gm Garlic (*lasan*), chopped
½ tsp / 2½ gm Ginger (*adrak*) paste (see p.191)
1 cup / 50 gm Spinach (*palak*), finely chopped
Salt to taste
Black peppercorns (*sabut kali mirch*) to taste, freshly ground
Lemon (*nimbu*) juice to taste

METHOD

- Melt 1 tsp butter in a pressure cooker; add onion and cook for a minute. Add the potatoes and cook for 30 seconds. Add 3 cups water and pressure cook till one whistle, cool, blend and strain.

- Melt 1 tsp butter in a pan; add cumin powder, garlic, ginger paste, and spinach. Cook for 30 seconds.

- Add boiled chickpeas, strained onion-potato mixture, salt and black pepper to taste ; bring to the boil, and simmer for 2 minutes.

- Add lemon juice to taste and serve hot.

- This is a wholesome soup with a good combination of proteins and carbohydrates.

- All soups taste best when served fresh.

CHICKPEA SALAD
Kabuli Chana Salaad

Serves: 4-6

INGREDIENTS

125 gm Chickpeas (*kabuli chana*), boiled, strained (see p. 193)

For the dressing:
1½ tbsp / 25 ml Lemon (*nimbu*) juice
2 tsp / 10 gm Sugar, powdered
1 tbsp Coriander (*dhaniya*) leaves, chopped
½ tsp / 2½ gm Salt
¼ tsp Red chilli flakes

For the tempering:
1 tbsp / 15 ml Vegetable oil
¼ tsp Mustard seeds
12 Curry leaves (*kadhi patta*)

For the garnishing:
2 tbsp / 30 gm Coconut (*nariyal*), grated
1 tbsp Coriander leaves, chopped

METHOD

- **For the dressing**, combine all the ingredients together.

- Mix the dressing with the boiled chickpeas. Cover with cling film and chill for an hour.

- **For the tempering**, heat 1 tbsp oil in a pan for 30 seconds; add mustard seeds and curry leaves. Pour over chilled salad, just before serving.

- Serve garnished with grated coconut and coriander leaves.

• This unusual salad, with the delicate flavour of coconut, is tempered with south Indian spices.

CORN SALAD
Makai Salaad

INGREDIENTS

1¾ / 175 gm Sweet corn
(*makai*)
½ cup / 50 gm Yellow capsicum,
chopped into medium cubes
½ cup / 50 gm Red capsicum,
chopped into medium cubes
¼ cup / 25 gm Spring onions
(*hara pyaz*), chopped
2 tsp / 10 ml Vegetable oil
½ cup / 25 gm Fried noodles
for garnishing

For the dressing:

1½ tbsp / 25 ml Vegetable oil
1 tbsp / 15 ml White / Balsamic
vinegar (*sirka*)
¼ tsp Salt
¼ tsp Black peppercorns (*sabut
kali mirch*), freshly ground
1 tsp / 5 gm Sugar, powdered

METHOD

- Heat 2 tsp oil in a pan; add the corn and cook for a minute. Keep aside to cool (see p. 197). Refrigerate corn and chopped vegetables till further use.

- **For the dressing**, mix all the ingredients together and keep aside.

- Mix the corn and vegetables with the dressing just before serving.

- Serve chilled garnished with fried noodles.

- Cut vegetables for salad should always be covered with cling film before chilling.
- Olive oil and refined groundnut oil can also be used for the dressing.
- Noodles are always deep-fried after boiling.

CUCUMBER SALAD WITH YOGHURT DRESSING
Dahi Kakdi

INGREDIENTS

2 / 300 gm Cucumber (*khira*), medium-sized

1 tbsp Peanuts (*moongphalli*), coarsely powdered (see p.185)

For the dressing:

½ cup / 100 gm Yoghurt (*dahi*), thick (see p. 198)

2 tsp / 10 ml White / Balsamic vinegar (*sirka*)

2 tsp / 10 gm Sugar, powdered

¼ tsp Salt

1 tsp Mint (*pudina*), chopped

METHOD

- Cut cucumber into slices and chill.
- **For the dressing**, mix all the ingredients together and refrigerate.
- Layer the dressing over the cucumber slices, just before serving.
- Serve chilled garnished with peanuts.

- Drain 1½ cups yoghurt and keep in a strainer for 20 minutes to get ½ cup thick yoghurt.
- Use baby cucumber or English cucumber for better taste.

POTATO AND PICKLED ONION SALAD
Aloo Pyaz, Sirkewale

INGREDIENTS

6 / 450 gm Potatoes, medium-sized

1¼ cups / 125 gm Pickled onions (see p. 164)

½ cup / 50 gm Spring onions (*hara pyaz*), chopped

1½ tbsp / 25 ml Vegetable oil

For the dressing: mix and keep aside

¾ tsp / 4 gm Salt

½ tsp / 2½ gm Black peppercorns (*sabut kali mirch*), freshly ground

2 tsp / 10 gm Sugar, powdered

2 tsp Mint (*pudina*) leaves, coarsely pounded

½ tsp / 2½ gm Mustard (*sarson*) powder

1 tbsp / 15 ml White / Balsamic vinegar (*sirka*)

½ tsp / 2½ gm Ginger (*adrak*) paste

2 tsp / 10 ml Lemon (*nimbu*) juice

For the garnishing:

1 tbsp Coriander (*dhaniya*) leaves, chopped

2 tbsp Peanuts (*moongphalli*), skinned

METHOD

• Apply ½ tbsp oil on the potatoes. Bake at 200° C / 400° F for 25-35 minutes or until soft (see p. 182). Peel and cut the potatoes into 1" cubes.

• Heat 1 tbsp oil in a pan; add the potatoes and sauté on medium heat till light golden brown. Remove and keep aside to cool.

• Mix the sautéed potatoes, pickled onions, and spring onions with the dressing, just before serving.

• Serve garnished with coriander leaves and peanuts.

• Baked and sautéed potatoes seasoned with *chaat masala* can be served as a tasty snack with drinks.

SALAD MEDLEY WITH JAGGERY DRESSING
Mila Jula Salaad

INGREDIENTS
2 / 300 gm Cucumber (*khira*),
medium-sized, cut into medium-
sized cubes
1 / 50 gm Carrot (*gajar*), cut
into medium-sized cubes
1 / 100 gm Tomato, cut into
medium-sized cubes
1 / 150 gm Apple (*seb*), cut into
medium-sized cubes
¼ cup / 25 gm Sweet corn
(*makai*)

For the dressing:
1 tbsp / 15 ml Vegetable oil
¼ tsp Red chilli flakes
2 tsp / 10 gm Jaggery (*gur*)
2 tsp / 10 ml Lemon (*nimbu*)
juice
¼ tsp Mint (*pudina*) powder
(see p. 11)
¼ tsp Salt

METHOD
* Cut the vegetables, cover
  with cling film, and chill in the
  refrigerator.

* **For the dressing**, heat 1 tbsp
  oil in a pan for 30 seconds.
  Add red chilli flakes and cook
  for 10 seconds. Add jaggery
  and mix well.

* Turn off the heat, and cool
  the mixture. Add lemon juice,
  mint powder, and salt;
  keep aside.

* Mix the dressing with the
  chilled vegetables and cut
  apple just before serving.

• Jaggery is made by boiling raw sugarcane juice and is used
  extensively in Indian cooking. It gives a unique flavour to the salad.

• Sprinkle 1 tsp lemon juice on cut apple to prevent browning.

SWEET POTATO AND BEAN SPROUT SALAD

Chatpata Shakarkandi Salaad

Serves: 4-6

INGREDIENTS

500 gm Sweet potatoes (*shakarkandi*)
25 gm Bean sprouts
100 gm Iceberg lettuce
1-2 tbsp / 15-30 ml Vegetable oil for shallow-frying
For the dressing: mix and keep aside
1½ tbsp / 25 ml Lemon (*nimbu*) juice
3 tsp / 15 gm *Chaat masala*
2 tbsp Coriander (*dhaniya*) leaves, chopped
½ tsp / 2½ gm Salt

METHOD

- Apply oil on the sweet potatoes. Bake at 200°C / 400°F for 20-30 minutes until soft (see p. 182). Peel and cut into ¼" discs.

- Heat 2 tbsp oil in a pan for 60 seconds and shallow-fry the discs on medium heat till light golden brown.

- Remove onto a plate.

- Add dressing just before serving.

- Arrange the discs on a serving plate and garnish with bean sprouts and lettuce.

- Applying oil on the sweet potatoes helps to peel the skin easily.
- Instead of baking, sweet potatoes can also be pressure cooked.
- Sweet potato discs with dressing can also be served as a starter.

TOMATO AND COTTAGE CHEESE SALAD
Tamatar aur Masala Paneer Salaad

Serves: 4-6

INGREDIENTS

4 / 400 gm Tomatoes, firm, medium-sized, quartered, pulp removed (see p.186)
125 gm Masala cottage cheese (*paneer*) (see p.189), cut into small cubes, chilled
4 Lettuce leaves, large

For the seasoning:
1 tbsp / 15 ml Olive / Vegetable oil
2 tsp / 10 ml White / Balsamic vinegar (*sirka*)
2 tsp / 10 gm Sugar, powdered
¼ tsp Mustard (*sarson*) powder
¼ tsp Mint (*pudina*) powder (see p. 11)
¼ tsp Black peppercorns (*sabut kali mirch*), freshly ground
¼ tsp Salt

METHOD

- **For the seasoning,** mix all the ingredients together.

- Apply ¾th of the seasoning on the tomato skins.

- Mix the remaining ¼th of the seasoning with the cubed masala cottage cheese.

- Arrange the seasoned tomato skins on a serving plate. Put 1 tbsp cottage cheese mixture on each tomato skin.

- Serve chilled garnished with a fan formation of lettuce leaves.

- Masala cottage cheese, cut into larger cubes, can also be served, along with toothpicks as a starter.

SNACKS & STARTERS

CORN ON TOAST
Karare Makai Pav

INGREDIENTS

4 Bread slices
¾ cup / 75 gm Sweet corn
(*makai*)
1 tbsp / 15 gm Celery, chopped
¼ cup / 50 gm White sauce
(see below)
Vegetable oil for deep-frying
Coriander (*dhaniya*) leaves
and Tomatoes, chopped for
garnishing

For the white sauce:

2 tsp / 10 ml Vegetable oil
1 tsp / 5 gm All purpose flour
(*maida*)
½ cup / 100 ml Milk
Salt and black pepper (*kali
mirch*) to taste
¼ tsp Sugar
2 tsp / 10 gm Processed cheese,
grated

METHOD

• **For the white sauce**, heat
  2 tsp oil in a pan for 30
  seconds; add flour and
  sauté for 10 seconds, turn
  off the heat. Add milk and
  the remaining ingredients of
  white sauce and mix well.
  Turn on the heat again and
  bring mixture to the boil,
  stirring constantly. Remove
  and keep aside.

• Mix the corn and celery in
  the white sauce and
  keep aside.

• Remove the sides of the
  bread and cut each slice into
  4 triangles.

• Heat 1"-deep oil in a shallow
  pan; deep-fry the bread
  triangles in hot oil till light
  golden brown. Remove with
  a slotted spoon.

• Put 1 tsp of corn mixture
  on each bread piece, garnish
  with tomatoes and coriander
  leaves and serve hot.

• Use a-day-old bread, as it absorbs less oil.
• Use milk at room temperature and be sure to turn off the heat, as
  instructed in the white sauce preparation, to avoid lumps.

• Calorie watchers can toast the bread instead of frying.
• This snack makes a good starter with drinks.
• Serve with tomato sauce and red chilli sauce.

CRISPY BABY CORN
Chhote Karare Bhutte

Serves: 4-6

INGREDIENTS

12 Baby corn (*bhutta*) kernels
Vegetable oil for deep-frying

For the batter:
2 tbsp / 30 gm All purpose flour (*maida*)
2 tbsp / 30 gm Corn flour
2 tsp / 10 gm White sesame (*til*) seeds
1 tbsp / 15 gm Celery, chopped
¼ tsp Baking powder
¼ tsp Black pepper (*kali mirch*)
¼ tsp Salt
¼ tsp Sugar
Water to make semi-thick batter

METHOD

• **For the batter,** mix all the ingredients mentioned and prepare a semi-thick batter with water.

• Coat each baby corn kernel with the prepared batter.

• Heat 1"-deep oil in a shallow pan; deep-fry baby corn in medium-hot oil, till light golden brown.

• Remove with a slotted spoon and serve hot.

• If the baby corn kernels are thick, slit them into two, vertically.
• This snack makes a good starter in parties.

• This snack can be half-fried ahead of time and re-fried for a minute in hot oil, just before serving.

COTTAGE CHEESE FRITTERS
Paneer Pakodi

INGREDIENTS

500 gm Cottage cheese
(*paneer*) (see p. 188), cut into 2"
X 2" block, ½" thick
Vegetable oil for deep-frying
Chaat masala to sprinkle

For the filling: mix together

3 tsp / 15 gm Ginger (*adrak*)
paste (see p. 191)
1½ tsp / 8 gm Green chilli
paste (see p. 191)
2 tsp / 10 gm Coriander
(*dhaniya*) paste
½ tsp / 2½ gm *Chaat* masala
¼ tsp Salt
1 tsp / 5 ml Lemon (*nimbu*)
juice mix

For the batter:

1½ cups / 150 gm Gram flour
(*besan*)
¼ tsp Baking powder
¼ tsp Carom (*ajwain*) seeds
½ tsp / 2½ gm Salt
125 ml Water (approx.) to
make semi-thick batter

METHOD

- Slit ½" -thick blocks of
  cottage cheese horizontally
  into 2 slices. Put ½ tsp layer
  of filling on one slice and
  cover with the second slice.

- **For the batter,** mix all the
  ingredients together and
  prepare a semi-thick batter
  with water.

- Press the filled 2 slices of
  cottage cheese together and
  coat with the batter on all
  sides. Heat 1"-deep oil in a
  shallow pan; deep-fry cottage
  cheese in medium-hot oil till
  light golden brown.

- Remove with a slotted
  spoon.

- Cut each into 2 pieces,
  place the cut side up on the
  serving plate, sprinkle *chaat*
  masala and serve hot.

- Use fresh cottage cheese.
- Serve as an appetizer to a meal or as a snack for high-tea.

FLORET FRITTERS
Gobi Pakodi

Serves: 4-6

INGREDIENTS

1 / 400 gm Cauliflower (*phool gobi*), medium-sized, cut into 20 florets
Vegetable oil for deep-frying
Chaat masala and Coriander (*dhaniya*) leaves, chopped for garnishing

For the batter:
1½ cups / 150 gm Gram flour (*besan*)
¼ tsp Baking powder
¾ tsp / 4 gm Carom (*ajwain*) seeds
$\frac{1}{8}$ tsp Asafoetida (*hing*)
¾ tsp / 4 gm Salt
2 tsp / 10 gm Ginger (*adrak*) paste (see p. 191)
1 tsp / 5 gm Green chilli paste (see p. 191)
2 tbsp Coriander leaves, chopped
1 tbsp / 15 gm Coriander (*dhaniya*) seeds, crushed
¾ cup / 150 ml Water (approx.) to make semi-thick batter

METHOD

- Boil 5 cups water, add ½ tsp salt and cauliflower florets and cook for a minute. Remove and drain.

- **For the batter,** mix all the ingredients together and prepare a semi-thick batter with water.

- Coat the cooked cauliflower florets with the batter. Heat 1"-deep oil in a shallow pan; deep-fry the florets

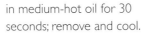

in medium-hot oil for 30 seconds; remove and cool.

- Press it slightly, re-fry in hot oil till light golden brown.

- Sprinkle *chaat* masala and coriander leaves. Serve hot.

- Make sure not to over boil the cauliflower as this will increase its oil absorption.
- Floret fritters are an excellent accompaniment to any meal and can also be served as a snack.
- Serve with green chutney (see p. 154) / sweet chutney (see p. 157) and tomato sauce.

POTATO FRITTERS
Aloo Pakodi

INGREDIENTS

2 / 150 gm Potatoes, medium-
sized, cut into round discs,
immersed in water
Vegetable oil for deep-frying
Chaat masala and Coriander
(*dhaniya*) leaves, chopped for
garnishing

For the batter:

1½ cups / 150 gm Gram flour
(*besan*)
½ tsp / 2½ gm Carom (*ajwain*)
seeds
a pinch Asafoetida (*hing*)
1 tsp / 5 gm Ginger (*adrak*) paste
(see p. 191)
½ tsp / 2½ gm Green chilli paste
(see p. 191)
½ tsp / 2½ gm Red chilli powder
½ tsp / 2½ gm Salt
¼ tsp Baking powder
¾ cup / 35 gm Fenugreek
(*methi*) leaves, chopped
125 ml Water (approx.) to
make semi-thick batter

METHOD

- **For the batter**, mix all the ingredients together and prepare a semi-thick batter.

- Coat the potato slices with the batter on both sides.

- Heat 1"-deep oil in a shallow pan; deep-fry the potato slices in medium-hot oil till light golden brown. Remove with a slotted spoon.

- Sprinkle *chaat* masala and coriander leaves, and serve hot.

- Serve with green chutney (see p. 154), sweet chutney (see p. 157) or tomato sauce.

- A perfect snack to eat with hot tea on a rainy afternoon.
- Potato fritters are quick to prepare when unexpected guests drop-in.

STUFFED CHILLI FRITTERS
Bharwa Mirchi ki Pakodi

INGREDIENTS

12 Light green chillies, large
Vegetable oil for deep-frying
Chaat masala and Coriander
(*dhaniya*) leaves, chopped for
garnishing

For the stuffing:
2 tsp / 10 ml Vegetable oil
1½ cups / 150 gm Sweet corn
(*makai*)
Salt to taste
½ tsp / 2½ gm *Chaat* masala
2 tbsp Coriander leaves,
chopped
½ tsp Mint (*pudina*) powder
(see p. 11)
1 tsp / 5 ml Lemon (*nimbu*) juice

For the batter
1½ cups / 150 gm Gram flour
(*besan*)
¼ tsp Baking powder
¼ tsp Carom (*ajwain*) seeds
a pinch Asafoetida (*hing*)
½ tsp / 2½ gm Salt
¾ cup / 150 ml Water to make
a semi-thick batter

METHOD

• **For the stuffing,** heat 2 tsp oil in a pan; add sweet corn, salt to taste, *chaat* masala, coriander leaves, and mint powder; cook for a minute. Add lemon juice and mix well. Keep aside.

• Slit each green chilli vertically with a sharp knife, keeping its shape intact. Fill with the corn stuffing.

• **For the batter,** mix all the ingredients together and prepare a semi-thick batter with water. Coat each chilli evenly with the batter.

• Heat 1"-deep oil in a shallow pan; deep-fry the green chillies in medium-hot oil till light golden brown. Remove with a slotted spoon.

• Sprinkle chaat masala and coriander leaves and serve hot.

• They can be semi-fried ahead of time, refrigerated and re-fried in hot oil before serving.

• Chillies can be filled with any stuffing of your choice.

SPICY SPINACH FRITTERS
Palak Chaat

INGREDIENTS

20 Spinach (*palak*), leaves
Vegetable oil for deep-frying

For the batter:
1 cup / 100 gm Gram flour (*besan*)
1½ tbsp / 25 gm Rice flour
½ tsp / 2½ gm Carom (*ajwain*) seeds
1 tsp / 5 gm Red chilli powder
a pinch Asafoetida (*hing*)
¼ tsp Baking powder
½ tsp / 2½ gm Salt
½ cup / 100 ml Water (approx.) to make semi-thick batter

For serving:
1 cup / 125 gm Potatoes, boiled, chopped (see p. 183)
½ cup / 100 gm Green chutney (see p. 154)
¾ cup / 150 gm Sweet chutney (see p. 157)
1¼ cups / 250 gm Yoghurt (*dahi*), beaten
Salt to taste
Red chilli powder to taste
Roasted cumin (*jeera*) powder to taste (see p. 184)
Thin *sev* and Coriander (*dhaniya*) leaves, chopped for garnishing

METHOD

• **For the batter,** mix all the ingredients together and prepare a semi-thick batter with water.

• Coat each spinach leaf with batter, on both sides.

• Heat 1"-deep oil in a shallow pan; deep-fry the spinach leaves in medium-hot oil to light golden brown. Keep aside.

• **For serving,** place 2 spinach fritters on an individual serving plate. Add 2 tsp chopped potatoes, 1 tsp green chutney, 2 tsp sweet chutney, and 1 tbsp yoghurt on each spinach fritter. Sprinkle salt, red chilli powder, and roasted cumin powder to taste. Garnish with thin *sev* and coriander leaves. Serve immediately.

• Spices can be adjusted as per taste
• This can also be served as a side dish at meal times.

• All *chaats* should be arranged just before serving, otherwise they tend to get soggy.

CRISPY LENTIL FINGERS
Mast Dal Paare

INGREDIENTS

¾ cup / 125 gm Green gram (*dhuli moong dal*), washed, soaked for 2 hours
2 tsp / 10 gm Ginger (*adrak*), chopped
2 tsp / 10 gm Green chillies, chopped
1½ cups / 300 ml Water for grinding
2 tbsp / 30 ml Vegetable oil
1½ tsp / 8 gm Cumin (*jeera*) seeds
½ tsp / 2½ gm Salt
2 tbsp Coriander (*dhaniya*) leaves, chopped
Vegetable oil for deep-frying

METHOD

• Drain the green gram and grind to a smooth paste with ginger, green chillies, and water.

• Heat 2 tbsp oil in a non-stick pan for a minute; add cumin seeds and turn off the heat when the seeds turn brown. Add the lentil paste, salt, and coriander leaves; mix well.

• Turn on the heat and cook the mixture, stirring constantly, till it leaves the sides of the pan.

• Pour the mixture, evenly, into a greased 8" square dish and cool it completely (3 hours). Cut into rectangular fingers 1½" x ½".

• Heat 1"-deep oil in a shallow pan; deep-fry the fingers in medium-hot oil till light golden brown. Serve hot.

• Turning off the heat after adding lentil paste is important otherwise the lentil mixture will become lumpy.
• Serve this snack in a party with a dip of your choice.

• The lentil mixture can be set ahead of time, refrigerated and fried when required.

DRY GREEN LENTIL
Sookhi Moong Dal

INGREDIENTS

¾ cup / 125 gm Green gram
(*dhuli moong dal*), soaked for 2
hours, drained
1 tbsp / 15 ml Vegetable oil
a pinch Asafoetida (*hing*)
1 tsp / 5 gm Cumin (*jeera*) seeds
1½ tsp / 8 gm Ginger (*adrak*)
paste (see p. 191)
1 tsp / 5 gm Green chilli paste
(see p. 191)
$^1/_8$ tsp Turmeric (*haldi*) powder
¾ cup / 150 ml Water (approx.)
Salt to taste

For the garnishing:
½ cup / 100 gm Tomatoes,
chopped
2 tbsp Coriander (*dhaniya*)
leaves, chopped

METHOD

- Heat 1 tbsp oil in a pan for 30 seconds; add asafoetida, cumin seeds, ginger and green chilli pastes, and turmeric powder; cook for 10 seconds.

- Add soaked lentil, ¾ cup water, and salt.

- Cook, covered, on low heat for 10-15 minutes or until done.

- Serve hot, garnished with tomatoes and coriander leaves.

- Be sure to reduce the flame while cooking since lentils loose water very rapidly.
- This can be served for all meals including breakfast.

- Serve with green chutney (see p. 154) and sweet chutney (see p. 157).

LENTIL PANCAKES
Moong Dal Cheela

INGREDIENTS

1¼ cups / 200 gm Green Gram
(*dhuli moong dal*), de-husked, split,
soaked for 2 hours, drained
2 tbsp / 30 gm Bengal gram
(*chana dal*), de-husked, split,
soaked for 2 hours, drained
2 tsp / 10 gm Green chillies,
chopped
2 tsp / 10 gm Ginger (*adrak*),
chopped
Salt to taste
a pinch Asafoetida (*hing*)
2 tbsp Coriander (*dhaniya*)
leaves, chopped
Vegetable oil for frying

For the filling:

1 cup / 150 gm Cottage cheese
(*paneer*), chopped (see p. 188)
2 tbsp Coriander leaves,
chopped
Salt to taste

METHOD

• Grind both the soaked lentils, green chillies, and ginger with
  minimum water to a smooth batter. Mix the batter with salt,
  asafoetida, and coriander leaves in a bowl. Keep aside.

• **For the filling**, mix all the ingredients together and keep aside.

• Heat a non-stick pan and brush with oil; add 1½ tbsp batter
  and spread until 6" wide. Add 2 tsp oil around the sides of the
  pancake and cook till light golden brown. Flip and leave for 30
  seconds. Flip again.

• Place 1 tbsp cottage cheese filling, fold and serve hot.

• This is a good breakfast dish, high in proteins and carbohydrates.
• It is served as an accompaniment at *chaat* parties.

• Calorie watchers can make oil-free pancakes.

SAVOURY LENTIL CAKES
Chatpata Dhokla

INGREDIENTS

1½ cups / 150 gm Gram flour (*besan*)
1 tsp / 5 gm Sugar
1 tsp / 5 gm Salt
1 tsp / 5 gm Citric acid
1 tbsp / 15 ml Vegetable oil
1 cup / 200 ml Water (approx.) to prepare the batter
1 tsp / 5 gm Baking soda (sodium bicarbonate)

For the tempering:

1 tbsp / 15 ml Vegetable oil
1 tsp / 5 gm Mustard seeds (*rai*)
5 Green chillies, slit
2 tbsp Coriander (*dhaniya*) leaves, chopped
¼ tsp Turmeric (*haldi*) powder
½ cup / 100 ml Water

For the garnishing:

2 tbsp / 30 gm Coconut (*nariyal*), grated
2 tbsp Coriander leaves, chopped

METHOD

- Place a greased 8" round steel container (empty) in a double boiler. While the container is being heated, mix gram flour, sugar, salt, citric acid, oil and prepare a batter with water. Add baking soda and keep stirring till it rises to double the quantity. Remove the container from the double boiler and put the batter into the container.

- Place the container back into the double boiler and cook, covered, on high heat for 10 minutes or until done (test with a toothpick). Remove the container from the double boiler and cool the mixture in the container itself. Cut into large cubes and temper (see below) within the container itself.

- **For the tempering**, heat 1 tbsp oil in a pan for 30 seconds; add mustard seeds, green chillies, coriander leaves, turmeric powder, and water. Bring to the boil, remove and pour over the prepared cubes.

- Garnish with coconut and coriander leaves and serve after a minimum of 15 minutes.

- To ensure lightness, add baking soda just before cooking.
- Insert a toothpick in the centre of the pan, if the mixture sticks to the toothpick, cook, covered, on low heat, for 5 more minutes.

- *Dokhla* can be served for breakfast or at tea time and is a favourite with the calorie watchers.
- Smear 2 tsp oil in a round steel container for greasing.

MUSHROOM CROQUETTES
Khumb ke Cutlet

Serves: 4-6

INGREDIENTS

1 / 125 gm Potato, large, boiled, grated
2 Bread slices
1½ tbsp / 25 gm Processed cheese, grated
¼ tsp Salt
Vegetable oil for deep-frying

For the filling:
2 tsp / 10 ml Vegetable oil
2 tbsp / 30 gm Mushrooms (*khumb*), chopped
1 tbsp / 15 gm Capsicum (*Shimla mirch*), chopped
Salt and black pepper (*kali mirch*) to taste

METHOD

- Dip the bread slices in water and squeeze (see p. 199). Mix bread, potato, cheese, and salt together. Keep aside

- **For the filling**, heat 2 tsp oil in the pan; add mushrooms, capsicum, salt and black pepper to taste. Cook for 30 seconds and remove.

- Divide the potato dough into 15 equal-sized balls. Stuff each ball with ¼ tsp filling, fold to seal the filling inside and reshape.

- Heat 1"-deep oil in a shallow pan; deep-fry the croquettes in medium-hot oil till light golden brown. Serve hot.

- The proportion of bread and potato has to be right otherwise the croquette will break while frying.

- Refrigerate after filling, to avoid cheese from fermenting.
- Deep-fry 3-4 croquettes at a time.

MUSHROOM CHEESE TOAST
Khumbi Toast

INGREDIENTS

1 French loaf, cut into 10 thin slanted slices
4 Button mushrooms (*khumb*), cut into thin vertical slices
1 / 75 gm Onion, medium-sized, chopped
2 tsp / 10 gm Soft butter
½ cup / 100 gm Cheddar cheese, grated
Salt and black pepper (*kali mirch*) to taste
1 / 100 gm Capsicum (*Shimla mirch*), medium-sized, chopped
Red chilli flakes to sprinkle

METHOD

- Apply soft butter on each slice of French loaf and place mushroom and onion slices along the length.

- Sprinkle cheese, salt and black pepper to taste. Garnish with capsicum and red chilli flakes.

- Bake at 180°C / 350°F for 5-8 minutes or until brown.

- Always pre-heat the oven for 15 minutes before baking.
- This makes a good starter with drinks.

- Mushroom cheese toast is a favourite among all kids.

TOASTED GARDEN SANDWICHES
Hara Bhara Toast

INGREDIENTS

12 Bread slices

For the filling:

6 Beans, cut into 1" pieces

1 / 150 gm Carrot (*gajar*),
medium-sized, cut into 1" pieces

1 cup / 100 gm Cabbage
(*bandh gobi*), cut into 1" pieces

6 Baby corn (*bhutta*) kernels,
cut into 1" pieces

1 / 100 gm Capsicum (*Shimla
mirch*), medium-sized, cut into
1" pieces

2 tsp / 10 gm Butter

Salt and black pepper (*kali
mirch*) to taste

2 tsp / 10 gm All purpose flour
(*maida*)

¼ cup / 50 ml Milk

Soft butter for applying on both
sides of the bread

METHOD

- **For the filling**, heat 2 tsp butter in a pan for 30 seconds; add all
  the cut vegetables, salt and black pepper to taste. Cook covered
  for a minute.

- Add flour to the vegetables and cook for 30 seconds. Add milk,
  cook for a further 30 seconds and keep aside.

- Pre-heat the toaster. Apply soft butter on one side of the bread
  slice. Take two slices of bread, place a portion of the filing on the
  buttered side and cover with the second slice, buttered
  side down.

- Apply butter on top surface of the sandwich, turn around and
  place sandwich in a toaster, now apply butter on the other
  surface.

- Close the toaster, and toast till golden brown.

- Garden sandwiches can be made with all kinds of bread – white,
  brown and multi-grain.
- This snack can be served for breakfast or high-tea with tomato sauce.

- Remove butter from fridge half an hour before preparing to get
  soft butter.

SAGO CUTLETS
Sabu Dana Vada

INGREDIENTS

½ cup / 75 gm Sago (*sabu dana*), washed, soaked, drained, kept covered for 8 hours
4 / 300 gm Potatoes, medium-sized boiled (see p. 183), peeled, grated
2 Bread slices, wet, squeezed (see p. 199)
2 tsp / 10 gm Ginger (*adrak*), chopped
½ tsp / 2½ gm Green chillies, chopped
2 tbsp Coriander (*dhaniya*) leaves, chopped
¼ cup Peanuts (*moongphalli*), skinned, coarsely powdered (see p. 185)
½ tsp / 2½ gm Salt
Vegetable oil for deep-frying

METHOD

• Mix the grated potato with sago, squeezed bread, ginger, green chillies, coriander leaves, powdered peanuts, and salt to a smooth mixture.

• Divide the mixture equally into 12-15 portions and shape into round, flat cutlets.

• Heat 1"-deep oil in a shallow pan; deep-fry the cutlets in hot oil till light golden brown and serve hot.

• Sago cutlets can be served with green chutney (see p. 154) and sweet chutney (see p. 157).

• Do not fry more than 3-4 cutlets at a time to avoid breaking
• Sago cutlets make an excellent party snack.

SPICY POTATO PATTIES
Chatpati Aloo Tikki

INGREDIENTS

10 / 750 gm Potatoes, boiled
(see p. 183), peeled, grated
2 Bread slices, wet, squeezed
(see p. 199)
1½ tbsp / 25 gm Corn flour
½ tsp / 2½ gm Salt
Vegetable oil for shallow-frying

For the filling:
1 cup / 100 gm Green peas
(*hara mattar*), boiled, ground
coarsely in a mixer
1 tbsp / 15 ml Vegetable oil
a pinch Asafoetida (*hing*)
¾ tsp / 4 gm Cumin (*jeera*)
seeds
1 tsp / 5 gm Ginger (*adrak*) paste
(see p. 191)
1 tsp / 5 gm Green chilli paste
(see p. 191)
1 tsp / 5 gm Red chilli powder
½ tsp / 2½ gm *Garam* masala
(see p. 184)
½ tsp / 2½ gm Mango powder
(*amchur*)
1 tbsp Coriander (*dhaniya*)
leaves, chopped
Salt to taste

METHOD

• **For the filling**, heat 1 tbsp
oil in a pan for 30 seconds;
add asafoetida, cumin seeds,
ginger paste, green chilli
paste, and ground green peas;
mix. Add red chilli powder,
garam masala, mango powder,
coriander leaves, and salt to
taste; cook on low heat for 2
minutes. Remove and keep
filling aside.

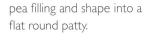

• Mix the potato, squeezed
bread, corn flour, and salt to a
smooth mixture.

• Divide the potato mixture
into 20 equal-sized balls. Stuff
each potato ball with 1 tsp

pea filling and shape into a
flat round patty.

• Shallow-fry the patties in hot
oil till light golden brown.
Serve immediately.

• Potato patties can be served with lunch and dinner as well as for
high-tea.

• Serve the patties with sweet chutney (see p. 157), green chutney
(see p. 154) and tomato sauce.

SPICY POTATO PRISMS
Samosa

INGREDIENTS

For the dough:

2½ cups / 250 gm All purpose flour (*maida*)

½ tsp / 2½ gm Salt

3 tbsp / 45 gm Clarified butter (*ghee*), melted

Lukewarm water to make the dough

Vegetable oil for deep-frying

For the stuffing:

4 / 400 gm Potatoes, medium-sized, boiled (see p. 183), peeled, coarsely mashed

1 tbsp / 15 ml Vegetable oil

a pinch Asafoetida (*hing*)

1 tsp / 5 gm Cumin (*jeera*) seeds

1 tsp / 5 gm Ginger (*adrak*) paste (see p. 191)

½ tsp / 2½ gm Green chilli paste (see p. 191)

3 tsp / 15 gm Coriander (*dhaniya*) powder

1 tsp / 5 gm Mango powder (*amchur*)

1 tsp / 5 gm Red chilli powder

½ tsp / 2½ gm *Garam* masala (see p. 184)

Salt to taste

2 tbsp Coriander (*dhaniya*) leaves, chopped

METHOD

- Sieve the flour and salt together. Add melted clarified butter and prepare a semi-hard dough with lukewarm water. Cover and keep aside for 10 minutes.

- **For the stuffing**, heat 1 tbsp oil in a pan for 30 seconds; add asafoetida, cumin seeds, ginger and green chilli pastes, and mashed potato; mix well. Add coriander powder, mango powder, red chilli powder, *garam* masala, salt to taste, and coriander leaves; mix well. Cook on low heat for 5 minutes, turning occasionally. Remove and cool.

- Divide the dough equally into 20 balls. Roll each ball, evenly, with a rolling pin, into a disc of 5" diameter and cut into half.

- Apply water on each semi-circle and make a hollow cone.

- Fill each cone with potato stuffing and seal the ends.

- Heat 1"-deep oil in a shallow pan; deep-fry the prisms in medium-hot oil till light golden brown and serve hot.

- To avoid bubbles in the flour covering of the *samosa*, fry in lukewarm oil first than turn up the heat after 2 minutes and deep-fry till light golden brown.

- *Samosa* is an all-time favourite snack amongst adults and children, alike.
- Serve with green chutney (see p. 154) and sweet chutney (see p. 157).

SAVOURY RICE FLAKES
Poha

INGREDIENTS

1 cup / 100 gm Beaten rice (*chiwda*), washed, drained in a colander
1-2 tbsp / 15-30 ml Vegetable oil
¼ tsp Mustard seeds (*rai*)
2 tsp / 10 gm Ginger (*adrak*), chopped
1 tsp / 5 gm Green chillies, chopped
12 Curry leaves (*kadhi patta*)
1 tbsp Raisins (*kishmish*), chopped
2 tbsp Cashew nuts (*kaju*), chopped
¾ cup / 75 gm Green peas (*hara mattar*), boiled
Salt to taste
½ tsp / 2½ gm Sugar
1 tsp / 5 ml Lemon (*nimbu*) juice
2 tbsp Coriander (*dhaniya*) leaves, chopped

METHOD

- Heat 1-2 tbsp oil in a pan for 30 seconds; add mustard seeds, ginger, green chillies, curry leaves, raisins, and cashew nuts. Cook for 30 seconds. Add green peas and cook for a minute.

- Add washed and drained beaten rice, salt to taste, sugar, lemon juice, and coriander leaves; mix well.

- Cook on low heat, covered, for 2 minutes. Serve hot.

- Savoury rice flakes is mainly served as a breakfast dish.
- Cashew nuts can be substituted with roasted peanuts.
- It can also be served along with toasted bread.

SAVOURY SEMOLINA CAKES
Rawa Idli

INGREDIENTS

1 cup / 150 gm Semolina (*rawa*),
dry roasted (see p. 185)
1½ cups / 300 gm Yoghurt
(*dahi*), sour
1 tsp / 5 gm Salt
1½ tbsp / 25 ml Vegetable oil
2 tsp / 10 gm Bengal gram
(*chana dal*), de-husked, split
2 tsp / 10 gm Black gram (*dhuli
urad dal*), de-husked, split
1 tsp / 5 gm Mustard seeds (*rai*)
2 tsp Curry leaves (*kadhi patta*),
chopped
1 tsp / 5 gm Baking soda
2 tbsp Coriander (*dhaniya*)
leaves, chopped
2 tsp / 10 ml Vegetable oil for
greasing

METHOD

• Mix the roasted semolina with yoghurt and salt to prepare a
batter.

• Heat 1½ tbsp oil in a pan; add both the lentils and cook till light
brown. Add mustard seeds and curry leaves; mix well. Remove
and mix with the semolina batter. Add baking soda and stir in the
batter. Mix well.

• Grease the semolina cake / *idli* stand with 2 tsp oil, add 1½ tbsp
batter to each mould and steam for 8-10 minutes or until done
(test, if cooked, with a toothpick / needle).

• Remove the semolina cakes with the help of a knife.

• Serve hot with coconut chutney (see p. 156).

• Baking soda should be added in the end, to ensure that *idlis* are light.
• For better taste use slightly sour yoghurt, preferably 1-2 days old.
• *Idli* stand is a stainless steel utensil with steaming compartments.

The stand is placed in a large vessel containing water to steam the
semolina or rice cakes.

SPICY SEMOLINA
Rawa Upma

INGREDIENTS

1 cup / 150 gm Semolina (*rawa*)
2 tbsp / 30 ml Vegetable oil
1 cup / 150 gm Onions, cut into medium-sized cubes
2 tsp / 10 gm Ginger (*adrak*), chopped
1 Green chilli, slit
2 tsp / 10 gm Bengal gram (*chana dal*), de-husked split
2 tsp / 10 gm Black gram (*dhuli urad dal*), de-husked, split
¾ tsp / 4 gm Mustard seeds (*rai*)
12 Curry leaves (*kadhi patta*)
2½ cups / 500 ml Water
Salt to taste
1 tbsp / 15 gm Clarified butter (*ghee*)
2 tbsp Coriander (*dhaniya*) leaves, chopped
1 tbsp / 15 ml Lemon (*nimbu*) juice
2 tbsp Peanuts (*moongphalli*), fried

METHOD

- Heat 1½ tbsp oil in a pan for 30 seconds; add onions, ginger, and green chilli. Cook till light brown. Add semolina and cook till light brown. Remove and keep aside.

- In the same pan, heat ½ tbsp oil; add the lentils and fry till light pink in colour. Add mustard seeds and curry leaves; mix well.

- Add 2½ cups water and salt to taste and bring to the boil. Add roasted semolina, little by little, stirring constantly. Cook till semi-thick.

- Add clarified butter, coriander leaves, lemon juice, and peanuts. Turn off the heat and leave covered for 2 minutes. Mix and serve hot.

- Spicy semolina is relished at breakfast or tea time with coconut chutney (see p. 156).
- Preparation of semolina with onion can be done much in advance.

- Seasoning with lentils and mixing with water should be done just before serving.

VEGETABLE VERMICELLI
Sabzdar Sewai

Serves: 2-4

INGREDIENTS

1 cup / 75 gm Vermicelli (*sewai*)
¼ tsp Clarified butter (*ghee*)
¼ cup / 50 gm Beans, cut diagonally into 1" pieces
¼ cup / 50 gm Carrot (*gajar*), cut diagonally into 1" pieces
2 tbsp / 30 ml Vegetable oil
½ tsp / 2½ gm Mustard seeds (*rai*)
1 tsp / 5 gm Bengal gram (*chana dal*), de-husked, split
1 tsp / 5 gm Black gram (*dhuli urad dal*), de-husked, split
2 tsp / 10 gm Ginger (*adrak*), chopped
1 tsp / 5 gm Green chillies, chopped
15 Curry leaves (*kadhi patta*)
1 cup / 100 gm Onions, sliced
1 cup / 200 ml Water
Salt to taste
2 tsp Coriander (*dhaniya*) leaves, chopped
1 tsp / 5 ml Lemon (*nimbu*) juice

METHOD

- Melt ¼ tsp clarified butter in a pan; add vermicelli and cook on low heat till light golden brown (see p. 185). Remove and keep aside.

- Boil 2½ cups water; add cut carrot and beans and cook for a minute. Remove and drain.

- Heat 2 tbsp oil in a pan for 30 seconds; add mustard seeds and both lentils, fry till light brown. Add ginger, green chillies, curry leaves, and onions; cook till light brown.

- Add roasted vermicelli, 1 cup water, and salt to taste. Mix well. Cook covered, on low heat, till the water evaporates.

- Add the vegetables, coriander leaves, and lemon juice. Mix and serve hot.

- Cook vermicelli in a flat pan for better texture.
- Soak the lentils in ½ cup water to soften. Drain before use.

- Serve with coconut chutney (see p. 156) or green chutney (see p. 154).

SPICY INDIAN PUFFS
Pani Puri

INGREDIENTS

For the puffs (puri):
50 gm Semolina (*rawa*)
50 gm All purpose flour (*maida*)
Water to make the dough
Vegetable oil for deep-frying

For the liquid filling:
2 / 250 gm Raw mangoes (*kairi*), medium-sized
2 cups Mint (*pudina*) leaves, chopped
1 tbsp / 15 gm Ginger (*adrak*), chopped
2 tsp / 10 gm Green chillies, chopped
4 cups / 800 ml Water
¼ tsp Asafoetida (*hing*)
1 tsp / 5 gm *Garam* masala (see p. 184)
4 Cloves (*laung*), roasted, powdered
2 tsp / 10 gm Roasted cumin (*jeera*) powder (see p. 184)
½ tsp / 2½ gm Red chilli powder
1 tbsp / 15 ml Lemon (*nimbu*) juice
Salt to taste
1 tsp / 5 gm Black salt (*kala namak*)

For the filling mixture:
1 cup / 125 gm Potatoes, boiled, chopped (see p. 183)
1 cup / 150 gm Horse gram (*kala chana*), boiled (see p. 192)
Salt, red chilli powder and cumin powder to taste
1 tbsp Coriander (*dhaniya*) leaves, chopped

METHOD

- **For the puffs (puri)**, sieve the semolina and flour together and prepare a semi-hard dough with water. Cover and keep aside for 15 minutes. Divide the dough equally into 50 balls and roll with a rolling pin into thin round discs of 1¼" diameter. Place the discs on a moistened cloth napkin and leave covered with another moistened cloth napkin for 30 minutes. Turn upside down holding the napkin edges.

- Heat 1"-deep oil in a shallow pan; deep-fry the discs in medium-hot oil, one at a time, till light golden brown. Remove, cool, store in an airtight jar for later use.

- **For the liquid filling**, pressure cook the mangoes with 2½ cups water to one whistle. Then simmer for 2 minutes. Remove and cool. Peel and mash the mangoes with the palm and discard seeds.

- Blend the mango pulp with mint, ginger, green chillies, and 4 cups water; strain. Add asafoetida, *garam* masala, roasted clove powder, cumin powder, red chilli powder, lemon juice, salt to taste, and black salt; stir well.

- To serve, mix together all the filling ingredients. Fill the puffs with 1 tsp filling mixture and pour liquid filling into the puff. Serve immediately.

- For a sweeter taste add 1 tsp sweet chutney (see p. 157) into the puff.

- *Pani puri* is a must for *chaat* parties.
- Ready-made puffs can often be bought from any Indian savoury store.
- Mango can be replaced with 2 cups of tamarind water (see p. 83).
- They are also known as *gol gappa* in North India and *puchka* in Eastern India.

SPICY CHAAT BOWLS
Chaat Katori

INGREDIENTS

2 cups / 250 gm All purpose flour (*maida*)

½ tsp / 2½ gm Salt

1 tbsp / 15 ml Vegetable oil

½ tsp / 2½ gm Carom (*ajwain*) seeds

Lukewarm water to make the dough

Vegetable oil for deep-frying

For the filling:

1¼ cups / 175 gm White peas (*safed mattar*), soaked for 6-8 hours, boiled (see p. 193)

2 / 150 gm Potatoes, medium-sized, boiled (see p. 183), peeled, chopped

1 cup Green chutney (see p. 154)

2 cups Sweet chutney (see p. 157)

2 cups / 400 gm Yoghurt (*dahi*), beaten (see p. 198)

Salt to taste

Red chilli powder and roasted cumin powder (see p. 184) to taste

Thin *sev* and Coriander (*dhaniya*) leaves chopped for decoration

20 Steel moulds (*katori*) (size 2¼")

METHOD

- Sieve the flour with salt. Add oil and carom seeds and prepare a hard dough with lukewarm water. Cover and keep aside for 10 minutes. Divide the dough into 20 equal balls. Roll each ball, evenly, with a rolling pin, into a disc of 4½" diameter.

- Stick each disc on the outer surface of a mould (*katori*), crimp the edges and prick with a fork.

- Heat 1"-deep oil in a shallow pan; fry in medium-hot oil for 2 minutes.

- Gently prise away the steel moulds from the flour base after 2 minutes. Continue to fry separated flour "bowl" (*chaat katori*) till light golden brown.

- To serve, take each flour bowl (*chaat katori*) and fill it with 1½ tbsp white peas, 1 tbsp chopped potatoes, 1 tsp green chutney, 2 tsp sweet chutney, and 1 tbsp beaten yoghurt. Sprinkle with salt, red chilli powder, and roasted cumin powder to taste and garnish with thin *sev* and coriander leaves. Serve immediately.

- You may vary the quantities of green chutney and sweet chutney to taste.
- This can be served for high-tea and at *chaat* parties.

- *Safed mattar* is also called *ragada* in Hindi.
- Remove the steel moulds (*katori*) with the help of tong and spoon when they are half done.

MAIN COURSE

YELLOW LENTIL
Arhar Dal

INGREDIENTS

1 cup / 150 gm Yellow lentil
(*arhar dal*), washed, soaked for
30 minutes
2 / 200 gm Tomatoes, medium-
sized, 1 grated, 1 roasted, peeled,
cut into cubes (see p. 186)
¾ tsp / 4 gm Salt
½ tsp / 2½ gm Turmeric (*haldi*)
powder
2 tsp / 10 gm Ginger (*adrak*),
chopped
2 tbsp Coriander (*dhaniya*)
leaves, chopped

For the tempering:

1 tbsp / 15 gm Clarified butter
(*ghee*)
a pinch Asafoetida (*hing*)
1 tsp / 5 gm Cumin (*jeera*) seeds
½ tsp / 2½ gm Red chilli powder

METHOD

- Pressure cook the soaked lentil with 1½ cups water, salt, and turmeric powder to one whistle and simmer for 4 minutes.

- Open the lid when the pressure drops, add the grated and cubed tomato, ginger, and coriander leaves; bring the mixture to the boil. Transfer to a serving bowl and season with the tempering.

- **For the tempering**, heat 1 tbsp clarified butter in a pan; add all the ingredients in the same order as mentioned (see p. 194). Remove and pour over the lentil. Serve hot.

- To give a fresh look to the lentil, always add the tempering just before serving.

- *Arhar dal* is also called *toor dal*, and is one of the most popular lentil used in Indian cuisine. It is the main ingredient of *sambar*.

BROWN LENTIL
Kale Masoor ki Dal

INGREDIENTS

1 cup / 150 gm Whole red lentil
(*kale masoor*), washed, soaked for
30 minutes
Salt to taste
½ tsp / 2½ gm Turmeric (*haldi*)
powder
¼ tsp Sugar
¼ *Garam* masala (see p. 184)
¼ tsp Mango powder (*amchur*)
2 tsp / 10 gm Ginger (*adrak*),
chopped
1 tbsp Coriander (*dhaniya*) leaves,
chopped

For the tempering:

1 tbsp / 15 gm Clarified butter
(*ghee*)
a pinch Asafoetida (*hing*)
¾ tsp / 4 gm Cumin (*jeera*) seeds
½ tsp / 2½ gm Red chilli powder

METHOD

- Pressure cook the soaked
  lentil with 2½ cups water, salt
  to taste, and turmeric powder
  to one whistle, simmer for 10
  minutes.

- Open the lid when the
  pressure drops. Add sugar,
  garam masala, mango powder,
  ginger, and coriander leaves;
  bring the mixture to the boil.
  Transfer to a serving bowl and
  season with the tempering.

- **For the tempering,** heat 1 tbsp
  clarified butter in a pan; add all
  the ingredients mentioned in
  the same order (see p. 194).
  Remove and pour over the
  lentil. Serve hot.

- Lentil is normally served at lunch time with one or two dry
  vegetables.

TEMPERED MIXED LENTIL
Dal Tarka

INGREDIENTS

$^1/_8$ cup Split green gram (*chilka moong dal*), washed, soaked for 30 minutes
$^1/_3$ cup / 50 gm Bengal gram (*chana dal*), de-husked, soaked for 30 minutes
½ cup / 75 gm Red gram (*malka masoor*), washed, drained
Salt to taste
¼ tsp Turmeric (*haldi*) powder
2 / 200 gm Tomatoes, medium-sized, roasted, de-skinned, cut into small cubes (see p. 186)
2 tsp / 10 gm Ginger (*adrak*), chopped
1 tsp / 5 gm Green chillies, chopped
¼ tsp Mango powder (*amchur*)
¼ tsp *Garam* masala (see p. 184)
1 cup / 50 gm Fenugreek (*methi*) leaves, chopped, cooked (see p. 196)
2 tbsp Coriander (*dhaniya*) leaves, chopped

For the tempering:
1 tbsp / 15 gm Clarified butter (*ghee*)
a pinch Asafoetida (*hing*)
½ tsp / 2½ gm Cumin (*jeera*) seeds
¼ tsp Red chilli powder

METHOD

• Pressure cook all the soaked lentils (see p. 192) with 2½ cups water, salt to taste, and turmeric powder to one whistle, simmer for 4 minutes.

• Open the lid when the pressure drops. Add chopped tomatoes, ginger, green chillies, mango powder, and *garam* masala; bring the mixture to the boil. Add cooked fenugreek and cook for a minute. Transfer to a serving dish and season with the tempering.

• **For the tempering,** heat 1 tbsp clarified butter in a pan; add all the ingredients mentioned in the same order (see p. 194). Remove and pour over the lentil. Serve hot.

• Red gram cooks very fast so avoid soaking it.

SPICED GREEN BANANAS IN YOGHURT CURRY
Kele ki Kadi

INGREDIENTS

2 Raw bananas (*kela*), medium-sized

1¼ cups / 250 gm Yoghurt (*dahi*), sour

1½ tbsp / 25 gm Gram flour (*besan*)

1½ cups / 300 ml Water

2 tbsp Coriander (*dhaniya*) leaves, chopped

For the basic seasoning:

2 tsp / 10 gm Clarified butter (*ghee*)

a pinch Asafoetida (*hing*)

¼ tbsp Fenugreek seeds (*methi dana*)

¼ Cumin (*jeera*) seeds

4 Dry red chillies (*sookhi lal mirch*)

½ tsp / 2½ gm Red chilli powder

½ tsp / 2½ gm Turmeric (*haldi*) powder

For the tempering:

1 tbsp / 15 gm Clarified butter

a pinch Asafoetida

¼ tsp Mustard seeds (*rai*)

6 Curry leaves (*kadhi patta*)

¼ tsp Red chilli powder

METHOD

- Pressure cook the bananas (see p. 183). Peel and cut into semi-circles.

- Mix the yoghurt with gram flour and 1½ cups water and make a smooth paste. Keep aside.

- **For the basic seasoning**, heat 2 tsp clarified butter in a pan for 30 seconds; add all the ingredients mentioned in the same order and mix.

- Add the cut bananas, yoghurt mixture, and salt; bring to the boil, stirring constantly. Reduce heat and simmer for 10 minutes.

- Add coriander leaves and transfer to a serving bowl and season with the tempering.

- **For the tempering**, heat 1 tbsp clarified butter in a pan; add all the ingredients mentioned in the same order (see p. 194). Pour over the prepared dish.

- Raw banana also called cooking banana is easily available in the vegetable market.

- This preparation can be served for both lunch and dinner.

DUMPLINGS IN SPICY YOGHURT SAUCE
Kadi Pakodi

INGREDIENTS

For the gram flour balls (*pakodi*):
1 cup / 100 gm Gram flour (*besan*)
2 tsp / 10 gm Ginger (*adrak*), chopped
1 tsp / 5 gm Green chillies, chopped
Vegetable oil for shallow-frying

For the yoghurt curry:
2 cups / 400 gm Yoghurt (*dahi*), sour
½ cup / 50 gm Gram flour
3½ cups / 700 ml Water

For the basic seasoning:
1 tbsp / 15 gm Clarified butter
a pinch Asafoetida (*hing*)
¼ tsp Fenugreek seeds (*methi dana*)
½ tsp / 2½ gm Cumin (*jeera*) seeds
4 Dry red chillies (*sookhi lal mirch*)
1 tsp / 5 gm Turmeric (*haldi*) powder
½ tsp / 2½ gm Red chilli powder

For the tempering:
1 tbsp / 15 gm Clarified butter
a pinch Asafoetida
½ tsp / 2½ gm Cumin seeds
¼ tsp Red chilli powder
1 tbsp Coriander (*dhaniya*) leaves, chopped

- This style of preparation is very typical of Uttar Pradesh, a state in north India. *Kadi pakodi* is always served with steamed rice.
- It is often served as a family treat on Sundays.
- 2-days-old refrigerated yoghurt is considered sour enough for this dish.

METHOD

- **For the gram flour balls (*pakodi*)**, prepare a semi-thick batter with gram flour and water. Add chopped ginger and green chillies. Beat till light and fluffy. (To test if the batter is fluffy drop ¼ tsp batter in ½ cup water, if batter floats it assures soft gram flour balls.)

- Heat ½"-deep oil in a shallow pan on medium heat; drop small portions of batter with your fingers and fry till light golden brown. Remove and immediately immerse in salted water; dip and remove. (For salted water, take 3¾ cups water and mix with 1½ tsp salt.)

- **For the yoghurt curry**, mix the yoghurt and gram flour with 3½ cups water to a smooth texture. Keep aside.

- **For the basic seasoning**, heat 1 tbsp clarified butter in a pan; add all the ingredients mentioned in the same order.

- Add the yoghurt mixture and salt to taste; bring to the boil. Add soaked gram flour balls and bring to the boil. Reduce heat and simmer for 15 minutes. Serve hot with the tempering.

- **For the tempering**, heat 1 tbsp clarified butter in a pan; add all the ingredients mentioned in the same order (see p. 194). Pour over the prepared dish.

- The process of dipping and removing the *pakodi* from water helps to remove the excess oil but still keeps it firm.

BENGAL GRAM WITH BOTTLE GOURD
Lauki Chane ki Dal

INGREDIENTS

¾ cup / 125 gm Bengal gram
(*chana dal*), de-husked, washed,
soaked for 30 minutes
1½ cups / 200 gm Bottle gourd
(*lauki*), peeled
2 tsp / 10 gm Ginger (*adrak*),
chopped
1 Green chilli, slit
Salt to taste
½ tsp / 2½ gm Turmeric (*haldi*)
powder
2 tbsp Coriander (*dhaniya*)
leaves, chopped
2 tsp / 10 ml Lemon (*nimbu*)
juice

For the tempering:

1 tbsp / 15 gm Clarified butter
(*ghee*)
a pinch Asafoetida (*hing*)
½ tsp / 2½ gm Cumin (*jeera*)
seeds
½ tsp / 2½ gm Red chilli
powder

METHOD

• Peel and cut bottle gourd into 1" cubes.

• Pressure cook the soaked lentil, bottle gourd, ginger, green chilli, salt to taste, and turmeric powder with 2 cups water, to one whistle; simmer for 10 minutes.

• Open the lid when the pressure drops. Add coriander leaves and bring the mixture to the boil. Reduce heat and simmer for 2 minutes. Add lemon juice and mix well. Transfer to a serving bowl and season with the tempering.

• **For the tempering**, heat 1 tbsp clarified butter in a pan; add all the ingredients in the same order mentioned (see p. 194). Pour over the prepared lentil.

• Avoid adding lemon juice while cooking, as the preparation may get bitter.
• Bengal gram and bottle ground compliment each other.

LENTIL DUMPLINGS & SPINACH IN YOGHURT SAUCE
Magori Palak ki Kadi

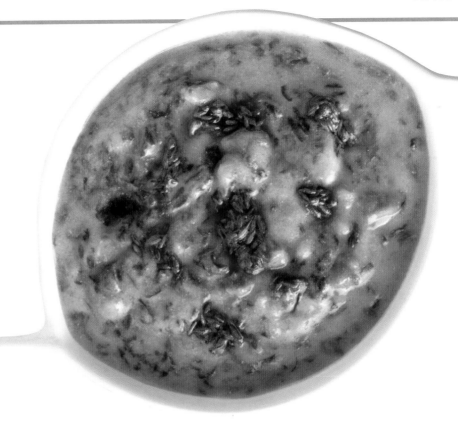

INGREDIENTS

1 cup / 100 gm Sun-dried green
gram dumplings (*magori*)
2 cups / 100 gm Spinach (*palak*),
chopped, cooked (see p. 196)
Vegetable oil for deep-frying
1½ cups / 300 gm Yoghurt
(*dahi*), sour
2 tbsp / 30 gm Gram flour
(*besan*)
1 tsp / 5 gm Ginger (*adrak*)
paste (see p. 191)
1 tsp / 5 gm Green chilli paste
(see p. 191)
1½ cups / 300 ml Water

For the seasoning:
½ tbsp / 8 gm Clarified butter
(*ghee*)
a pinch Asafoetida (*hing*)
1 tsp / 5 gm Cumin (*jeera*) seeds
¾ tsp / 4 gm Turmeric (*haldi*)
powder
½ tsp / 2½ gm Red chilli
powder

For the tempering:
1 tbsp / 15 gm Clarified butter
a pinch Asafoetida
¼ tsp Cumin seeds
¼ tsp Red chilli powder

METHOD

- Heat ½" deep oil in a shallow pan; deep-fry the *magori* in medium-hot oil till light golden brown. Remove, crush them lightly and keep aside.

- Mix yoghurt, gram flour, ginger paste, and green chilli paste with water to a smooth paste; keep aside.

- **For the seasoning,** heat the pressure cooker for 30 seconds; add ½ tbsp clarified butter and the remaining ingredients in the same order; mix. Add fried and crushed *magori*; mix. Add 1½ cups water and ¼ tsp salt; cook to one whistle, and simmer for 5 minutes. Turn off the heat.

- Open the lid when the pressure drops. Add yoghurt mixture and salt to taste; bring to the boil. Reduce heat and simmer for 10 minutes.

- Add cooked spinach and bring to the boil. Remove and transfer to a serving bowl and season with the tempering.

- **For the tempering,** heat 1 tbsp clarified butter in a pan; add all the ingredients in the same order mentioned (see p. 194). Pour over the prepared dish.

- *Magoris* are prepared by soaking and grinding split green gram, shaping into small dumplings and then drying them in the sun. They are available in food stores.

- Mix spinach just before serving as this gives a fresh appetizing look.
- Mash the cooked spinach before adding.

SPLIT GREEN LENTIL WITH SPINACH
Moong Dal Palak

INGREDIENTS

1 cup / 150 gm Green gram
(*moong dal*), washed, soaked for
15 minutes
1½ cups / 75 gm Spinach
(*palak*), chopped, cooked
(see p. 196)
¼ tsp Clarified butter (*ghee*)
Salt to taste
½ tsp / 2½ gm Turmeric (*haldi*)
powder
1½ tsp / 8 gm Ginger (*adrak*),
chopped
1 / 100 gm Tomato, medium-
sized, chopped

For the tempering:

1 tbsp / 15 gm Clarified butter
a pinch Asafoetida (*hing*)
1 tsp / 5 gm Cumin (*jeera*) seeds
2 Cloves (*laung*)
¼ tsp Black pepper (*kali mirch*)

METHOD

• Heat the pressure cooker for 30 seconds; add ¼ tsp clarified
butter, green gram, salt to taste, turmeric powder, ginger, tomato,
cooked spinach and 2 cups water. Cook to one whistle, remove
from heat.

• Open the lid when the pressure drops. Bring the mixture to the
boil. Transfer to a serving dish and season with the tempering.

• **For the tempering,** heat 1 tbsp clarified butter in the pan; add all
the ingredients in the same order mentioned (see p. 194). Pour
over the lentil. Serve hot.

• Green gram cooks very fast, so to avoid getting it soggy the pressure
has to be monitored.

• It can be served to patients who are advised an iron-rich diet and
light food.

CURRIED KIDNEY BEANS
Rajmah

INGREDIENTS

1 cup / 175 gm Kidney beans
(*rajmah*), washed, soaked for 8
hours
½ tsp / 2½ gm Salt
1 tsp / 5 gm Turmeric (*haldi*)
powder (¾ + ¼)
3 tbsp / 45 ml Vegetable oil
2 Bay leaves (*tej patta*)
2 Black cardamom (*badi elaichi*),
crushed
3 / 225 gm Onions, medium-
sized, grated
2 tsp / 10 gm Ginger (*adrak*)
paste (see p. 191)
½ tsp / 2½ gm Green chilli
paste (see p. 191)
¼ tsp Garlic (*lasan*) paste
(see p. 191)
¾ tsp / 4 gm Red chilli powder
4 / 400 gm Tomatoes, large,
liquidized (see p. 187)
½ tsp / 2½ gm *Garam* masala
(see p. 184)
2 tbsp Coriander (*dhaniya*)
leaves, chopped

METHOD

- Pressure cook the soaked beans with 4½ cups water, salt, and
  ¼ tsp turmeric powder to one whistle. Reduce heat and simmer
  for 30 minutes. Turn off the heat.

- Heat 3 tbsp oil in a pan for 30 seconds; add bay leaves, black
  cardamom, onions, ginger, green chilli and garlic pastes; fry until
  light golden brown. Add ¾ tsp turmeric powder and red chilli
  powder; mix.

- Add liquidized tomato and fry until oil separates.

- Add cooked kidney beans along with the water and salt to taste;
  bring to the boil. Reduce heat and simmer for 10 minutes.

- Add coriander leaves and *garam* masala. Turn off the heat.
  Serve hot.

- Curried kidney beans tastes best with steamed rice.
- This is a popular north Indian dish.
- 2 tsp clarified butter can also be added to the dish to enhance the
  flavour.

- Beans are available in two colours, light brown and dark brown. The
  dark brown ones take 10 minutes more to pressure cook than the
  light brown ones.

FENUGREEK FLAVOURED LENTIL
Urad Chana aur Methi Dal

INGREDIENTS

½ cup / 75 gm Split black gram
(*dhuli urad dal*), de-husked
⅓ cup / 50 gm Bengal gram
(*chana dal*), de-husked, split
Salt to taste
¾ tsp / 4 gm Turmeric (*haldi*)
powder
2 tsp / 10 gm Ginger (*adrak*),
chopped
1 tsp / 5 gm Green chillies,
chopped
1 cup / 50 gm Fenugreek (*methi*)
leaves, chopped
1 tsp / 5 gm Clarified butter
(*ghee*)
3 / 300 gm Tomatoes, medium-
sized, liquidized (see p. 187)
1½ cups / 300 ml Water
For the tempering:
1 tbsp / 15 gm Clarified butter
a pinch Asafoetida (*hing*)
1 tsp / 5 gm Cumin (*jeera*) seeds
½ tsp / 2½ gm Red chilli
powder

METHOD

- Wash and soak both the lentils together for 30 minutes. Pressure cook with salt to taste, turmeric powder, ginger, green chillies, and 1½ cups water to one whistle. Reduce heat and simmer for 4 minutes. Turn off the heat.

- Heat the pan for 30 seconds; add fenugreek leaves and cook covered for 30 seconds. Keep aside.

- Heat 1 tsp clarified butter in a pan for 30 seconds; add liquidized tomato and salt to taste; cook for 2 minutes on medium heat. Remove and keep aside.

- Add cooked fenugreek and tomato to the cooked lentil and bring the mixture to the boil. Remove and transfer to a serving bowl and season with tempering.

- **For the tempering**, heat 1 tbsp clarified butter in a pan; add all the ingredients in the same order mentioned (see p. 194). Pour over the lentil. Serve hot.

- Ensure that the tempering does not burn. To avoid this from happening remove the pan from the heat after adding asafoetida and cumin seeds. Add red chilli powder later.

SPICY GREEN LENTIL
Sabut Moong ki Dal

INGREDIENTS

1 cup / 150 gm Whole green gram (*sabut moong dal*), washed, soaked for 30 minutes
¾ tsp / 4 gm Turmeric (*haldi*) powder
Salt to taste
1 tbsp / 15 gm Ginger (*adrak*) chopped
1 Green chilli, slit
½ cup / 100 gm Tomatoes, grated (see p. 186)
½ tsp / 2½ gm Mango powder (*amchur*)
½ tsp / 2½ gm Sugar
¼ tsp Garam masala (see p. 184)
2 tbsp Coriander (*dhaniya*) leaves, chopped

For the tempering:

1½ tbsp / 25 gm Clarified butter (*ghee*)
a pinch Asafoetida (*hing*)
1 tsp / 5 gm Cumin (*jeera*) seeds
¾ tsp / 4 gm Red chilli powder

METHOD

- Pressure cook the soaked lentil with 3 cups water, turmeric powder, salt to taste, ginger, and green chilli to one whistle. Reduce heat and simmer for 12 minutes. Turn off the heat.

- Open the lid when the pressure drops. Add grated tomato, mango powder, sugar, *garam* masala, and coriander leaves; bring the mixture to the boil. Remove and transfer to a serving dish. Season with the tempering.

- **For the tempering**, heat 1½ tbsp clarified butter in a pan; add all the ingredients mentioned in the same order (see p. 194). Remove and pour over the lentil Serve hot.

- This lentil can be served with *besan methi roti* (see p. 138) and *khasta roti* (see p. 139).
- It is high in protein.
- Soaking the lentil for 30 minutes helps the lentil to cook faster.

POTATOES AND CAPSICUM
Aloo Shimla Mirch

INGREDIENTS

2 / 150 gm Potatoes, medium-sized, boiled (see p. 183) peeled, cut lengthwise into fingers
1 / 100 gm Capsicum (*Shimla mirch*), medium-sized, cut lengthwise into fingers
1½ tbsp / 25 ml Vegetable oil
a pinch Asafoetida (*hing*)
½ tsp / 2½ gm Cumin (*jeera*) seeds
2 tsp / 10 gm Gram flour (*besan*)
2 tsp / 10 gm Coriander (*dhaniya*) powder
½ tsp / 2½ gm Red chilli powder
Salt to taste

METHOD

• Heat 1 tbsp oil in a pan for 30 seconds; add asafoetida, cumin seeds, and gram flour; cook for 10 seconds.

• Add cut capsicum and cook for a minute. Add cut potatoes, coriander powder, red chilli powder, and salt to taste; cook on low heat for 2 minutes, stirring occasionally. Serve hot.

• Gram flour gives a unique flavour to this dish.
• All varieties of bell peppers can be used.

TAMARIND FLAVOURED POTATOES
Imli Aloo

INGREDIENTS

6 / 500 gm Potatoes, medium-sized, boiled (see p. 183), peeled, cut into 1" cubes
2 tbsp / 30 ml Vegetable oil
a pinch Asafoetida (*hing*)
1 tsp / 5 gm Cumin (*jeera*) seeds
¼ tsp Fenugreek seeds (*methi dana*)
¼ tsp Fennel (*saunf*) seeds
4 Dry red chillies (*sookhi lal mirch*)
1 tbsp / 15 ml Tamarind (*imli*) water (see below)
3 tsp / 15 gm Coriander (*dhaniya*) powder
1 tsp / 5 gm Red chilli powder
½ tsp / 2½ gm *Garam* masala (see p. 184)
½ tsp / 2½ gm *Chaat* masala
½ tsp / 2½ gm Mint (*pudina*) powder (see p. 11)
3 tbsp Coriander (*dhaniya*) leaves, chopped
Salt to taste

METHOD

- Heat 2 tbsp oil in a pan for 30 seconds; add asafoetida, cumin seeds, fenugreek seeds, fennel seeds, dry red chillies and tamarind water; cook for 30 seconds. Add potatoes and mix well.

- Add coriander powder, red chilli powder, *garam* masala, *chaat* masala, mint powder, coriander leaves, and salt to taste. Mix well. Cook on low heat for 5 minutes, stirring occasionally. Serve hot.

- *Imli aloo* can be enjoyed as a starter as well.
- Soak 1 tbsp tamarind in ½ cup hot water for 30 minutes, mash and strain in a bowl. Discard the seeds and use the tamarind water as required.

POTATOES AND PEAS
Sukhe Aloo Mattar

INGREDIENTS

4 / 300 gm Potatoes, medium-sized, boiled (see p. 183), peeled, cut into 1" cubes
½ cup / 50 gm Green peas (*hara mattar*), boiled
2 tbsp / 30 ml Vegetable oil
a pinch Asafoetida (*hing*)
1 tsp / 5 gm Cumin (*jeera*) seeds
¾ tsp / 4 gm Ginger (*adrak*) paste (see p. 191)
¼ tsp Turmeric (*haldi*) powder
½ tsp / 2½ gm Red chilli powder
2 / 200 gm Tomatoes, medium-sized, grated (see p. 186)
2 tsp / 10 gm Coriander (*dhaniya*) powder
Salt to taste
¼ tsp *Garam* masala (see p. 184)
2 tbsp Coriander (*dhaniya*) leaves, chopped
¼ tsp Cumin seeds
Salt and black pepper (*kali mirch*) to taste

METHOD

- Heat 1½ tbsp oil in a pan for 30 seconds; add asafoetida, cumin seeds, ½ tsp ginger paste, turmeric powder, red chilli powder, and grated tomato; cook until oil separates. Add cut potatoes and mix well.

- Add coriander powder, salt to taste, *garam* masala, and coriander leaves; cook for 5 minutes on low heat, stirring occasionally. Keep aside.

- Heat ½ tbsp oil in a pan for 30 seconds; add cumin seeds, ¼ tsp ginger paste, green peas, salt and black pepper to taste; cook on low heat for 2 minutes.

- Mix with prepared potatoes. Serve hot.

- To retain the green colour of the peas, it is advised to cook it separately from potatoes.

- Over cooking of greens generally changes the colour.

SESAME POTATOES
Til Aloo

INGREDIENTS

20 / 750 gm Baby potatoes, washed, wiped, make a cross with a sharp knife
2 tsp / 10 gm White sesame (*til*) seeds
2 tbsp / 30 ml Vegetable oil
½ tsp / 2½ gm Cumin (*jeera*) seeds
½ tsp / 2½ gm Ginger (*adrak*) paste (see p. 191)
½ tsp / 2½ gm Green chilli paste (see p. 191)
1 tsp / 5 gm Mint (*pudina*) paste
a pinch Asafoetida (*hing*)
½ tsp / 2½ gm *Chaat* masala
2 tbsp Coriander (*dhaniya*) leaves, chopped

For the stuffing: mix and keep aside

2 tsp / 10 gm Coriander (*dhaniya*) powder
¾ tsp / 4 gm Red chilli powder
1 tsp / 5 gm Mango powder (*amchur*)
½ tsp / 2½ gm *Garam* masala (see p. 184)
Salt to taste

METHOD

- Heat the pan for 30 seconds; add sesame seeds and roast on low heat, stirring constantly, till light brown. Keep aside.

- Pressure cook the potatoes, placing them in a container inside the pressure cooker filled with 1½ cups water, to one whistle. Reduce heat and simmer for 4 minutes. Remove and cool.

- Fill the boiled potatoes with the stuffing masala.

- Heat 2 tbsp oil in a pan for

30 seconds; add cumin seeds, ginger paste, green chilli paste, mint paste, stuffed potatoes, and *chaat* masala; cook on medium heat for 2 minutes, stirring constantly.

- Add coriander leaves and roasted sesame seeds; mix well. Serve hot.

- Instead of pressure cooking, potatoes can also be baked at 200°C / 400°F for 20-25 minutes or until soft, and can also be cooked in a microwave.

- Roasted sesame seeds give a nice crunchy taste to this dish..

MINTY POTATOES
Pudina Aloo

INGREDIENTS

400 gm Baby potatoes, boiled, peeled (see p. 183)
1½ tbsp / 25 ml Vegetable oil
a pinch Asafoetida (*hing*)
½ tsp / 2½ gm Cumin (*jeera*) seeds
1½ tsp / 8 gm Ginger (*adrak*) paste (see p. 191)
½ tbsp / 8 gm Green chilli paste (see p. 191)
1 tsp / 5 gm Mint (*pudina*) paste
2 tsp / 10 gm Coriander (*dhaniya*) powder
¾ tsp / 4 gm Red chilli powder
½ tsp / 2½ gm Mango powder (*amchur*)
1 tsp / 5 gm Mint powder (see p. 11)
¼ tsp *Chaat* masala
¼ tsp *Garam* masala (see p. 184)
3 tbsp Mint, chopped
2 tbsp Coriander (*dhaniya*) leaves, chopped
Salt to taste

METHOD

- Heat 1½ tbsp oil in a pan for 30 seconds; add asafoetida, cumin seeds, ginger paste, green chilli paste, and mint paste; cook for 10 seconds.

- Add potatoes and mix well. Add coriander powder, red chilli powder, mango powder, mint powder, *chaat* masala, and *garam* masala; cook on low heat for 5 minutes, turning occasionally.

- Add mint, coriander leaves and salt to taste; mix and cook for a minute. Serve hot.

- A combination of dry and fresh mint paste makes this dish delicious.

CUMIN POTATOES
Jeera Aloo

INGREDIENTS

4 / 300 gm Potatoes, medium-
sized, boiled (see p. 183), peeled,
cut into 1" cubes
1½ tbsp / 25 ml Vegetable oil
a pinch Asafoetida (*hing*)
½ tsp / 2½ gm Cumin (*jeera*)
seeds
2 tsp / 10 gm Coriander
(*dhaniya*) powder
½ tsp / 2½ gm Red chilli
powder
½ tsp / 2½ gm Mango powder
(*amchur*)
Salt to taste
2 tbsp Coriander (*dhaniya*)
leaves, chopped

METHOD

- Heat 1½ tbsp oil in a pan for
  30 seconds; add asafoetida
  and cumin seeds.

- Add cubed potatoes,
  coriander powder, red chilli
  powder, mango powder, and
  salt to taste; mix well. Cook
  on low heat for 5 minutes,
  turning occasionally.

- Add coriander leaves and
  cook for 30 seconds more.
  Serve hot.

- Cumin potatoes is a popular dish. It is quick to prepare and can be
  served with any meal.

CAULIFLOWER AND POTATOES
Gobi Aloo

Serves: 4-6

INGREDIENTS

1 / 400 gm Cauliflower (*phool gobi*), medium-sized, cut into 1½" florets

2 / 150 Potatoes, medium-sized, peeled, cut lengthwise into ½" pieces

1½ tbsp / 25 ml Vegetable oil

a pinch Asafoetida (*hing*)

½ tsp / 2½ gm Cumin (*jeera*) seeds

2 tsp / 10 gm Ginger (*adrak*), chopped

1 tsp / 5 gm Green chillies, chopped

¼ tsp Turmeric (*haldi*) powder

½ tsp / 2½ gm Red chilli powder

Salt to taste

½ tsp / 2½ gm *Garam* masala (see p. 184)

¼ tsp Mango powder (*amchur*)

1 tbsp Coriander (*dhaniya*) leaves, chopped

METHOD

- Heat 1½ tbsp oil in a heavy-bottom vessel for 30 seconds; add asafoetida, cumin seeds, ginger, chillies, turmeric powder, and red chilli powder; mix.

- Add cut potatoes, cauliflower, salt to taste, and ½ cup water. Cook, covered, on high heat, stirring occasionally, until the water dries up or the potatoes are cooked.

- Add *garam* masala, mango powder, and coriander leaves; mix well. Serve hot.

- Cut potatoes should be kept in water otherwise they turn brown.
- This preparation can be served for both lunch and dinner.

- In case water dries up while cooking, and the potatoes are still not done, it is advised to cook for 5 more minutes, covered, on low heat.

SPICY COLOCASIA
Sookhi Arvi

INGREDIENTS

250 gm Colocasia (*arvi*)
1½ tbsp / 25 ml Mustard oil / Vegetable oil
a pinch Asafoetida (*hing*)
½ tsp / 2½ gm Carom (*ajwain*) seeds
2 tsp / 10 gm Coriander (*dhaniya*) powder
½ tsp / 2½ gm Red chilli powder
¼ tsp Mango powder (*amchur*)
Salt to taste
2 tbsp Coriander (*dhaniya*) leaves, chopped.

METHOD

- Pressure cook the colocasia with water to one whistle. Cool and drain.

- Peel and press colocasia within the palm. Keep aside.

- Heat 1½ tbsp oil in a pan for 30 seconds; add asafoetida, carom seeds, and colocasia; mix well.

- Add coriander powder, red chilli powder, mango powder, and salt to taste. Cook on low heat for 5 minutes, turning occasionally. Add coriander leaves; mix. Serve hot.

- Colocasia is sticky by nature so avoid over boiling.

- In north India, only a few dishes are cooked in mustard oil for its unique flavour.

ROASTED SPICED EGGPLANT
Baingan Bharta

Serves: 4-6

INGREDIENTS

1 / 500 gm Eggplant (*baingan*), large, round, make 4 1" deep slits
2 tbsp / 30 ml Vegetable oil + 1 tsp for applying
1 / 100 gm Onion, large, cut into medium-sized cubes
1½ tsp / 8 gm Ginger (*adrak*), chopped
1 tsp / 5 gm Green chillies, chopped
½ cup / 50 gm Green peas (*hara mattar*), boiled
Salt to taste
2 / 200 gm Tomatoes, medium-sized, 1 grated (see p. 186), 1 chopped into 8 pieces
¼ tsp Turmeric (*haldi*) powder
½ tsp / 2½ gm Red chilli powder
1 tbsp Coriander (*dhaniya*) leaves, chopped

METHOD

- Apply 1 tsp oil on the outer surface of the eggplant. Roast over the flame until soft. Cool, peel, and mash. Keep aside.

- Heat 1 tbsp oil in a pan; add onion, ginger, and green chillies; cook until light brown. Add green peas and salt to taste; cook for a minute. Add cut tomato and cook for 30 seconds. Remove.

- Heat 1 tbsp oil in the same pan; add turmeric powder, red chilli powder, and grated tomato; cook for a minute. Add mashed eggplant and salt to taste; cook until semi thick.

- Add the onion mixture and coriander leaves; mix lightly for a minute. Serve hot.

- Applying oil on the outer surface of the eggplant helps to remove the skin easily.
- Roasting the eggplant enhances the flavour of the preparation.

CRISPY EGGPLANT
Chatpate Baingan

INGREDIENTS

1 / 300-400 gm Eggplant
(*baingan*), round, cut into ¼"-
thick slices
½ tsp / 2½ gm Salt
½ tsp / 2½ gm Turmeric (*haldi*)
powder
3-4 tbsp / 45-60 ml Vegetable oil
Chaat masala and Coriander
(*dhaniya*) leaves, chopped

**For coating the eggplant: mix
and keep aside**

2 tbsp / 30 gm Wholewheat
flour (*atta*)
½ tsp / 2½ gm Salt
½ tsp / 2½ gm Red chilli powder
2 tsp / 10 gm Sesame (*til*) seeds
½ tsp / 2½ gm Fennel (*saunf*)
powder
¼ tsp *Garam* masala (see p. 184)

METHOD

- Sprinkle ½ tsp salt and ½ tsp
  turmeric powder on both
  sides of the eggplant and leave
  aside for 10 minutes. Use later
  for coating.

- Coat each slice of eggplant
  with coating mixture, on both
  sides, evenly.

- Heat 2 tbsp oil in a non-stick
  pan for 30 seconds; add 5-6
  coated eggplant slices and
  cook until light golden brown
  on both sides, adding more oil
  if required. Repeat with the
  remaining slices.

- Serve hot, sprinkled with *chaat*
  masala and coriander leaves.

- Crispy eggplant can be prepared for any meal.
- Sprinkling salt and turmeric powder on the eggplant slices leaves water after
  10 minutes, and hence aids in binding the coating and eggplant together.

OKRA WITH PEARL ONIONS
Bhindi aur Chhote Pyaz

INGREDIENTS

250 gm Okra (*bhindi*), remove head and tail, cut diagonally to ¾" pieces
100 gm Baby onions, peeled
2 tbsp / 30 ml Vegetable oil
Salt to taste
1 tbsp Coriander (*dhaniya*) leaves, chopped
¼ tsp Sugar
2 Green chillies, medium-sized, cut diagonally
¼ tsp Black pepper (*kali mirch*)

METHOD

• Heat 1 tbsp oil in a pan for 30 seconds; add the onions and fry until light brown. Add salt to taste and coriander leaves; mix and keep aside.

• Heat 1 tbsp oil in the same pan for 30 seconds; add okra, salt to taste, sugar, and green chillies. Cook, covered, on low heat until soft.

• Add black pepper and onion mixture; cook for a minute. Remove and transfer into a serving dish.

• Adding ¼ tsp sugar while cooking okra helps to retain the green colour.

STUFFED OKRA
Bharwa Bhindi

Serves: 2-4

INGREDIENTS

250 gm Okra (*bhindi*), washed, wiped dry with a clean napkin

For the stuffing:

½ tsp / 2½ gm Turmeric (*haldi*) powder

2 tsp / 10 gm Coriander (*dhaniya*) powder

1 tsp / 5 gm Red chilli powder

2 tsp / 10 gm Fennel (*saunf*) powder

¾ tsp / 4 gm Mango powder (*amchur*)

Salt to taste

For the seasoning:

2½ tbsp / 40 ml Vegetable oil

a pinch Asafoetida (*hing*)

1 tsp / 5 gm Cumin (*jeera*) seeds

METHOD

- Cut the top and bottom of the okra and slit vertically with a sharp knife, keeping the shape intact

- Mix the stuffing ingredients together; fill each okra evenly.

- Heat 2½ tbsp oil in a pan for 30 seconds; add asafoetida, cumin seeds, and stuffed okra; cook, covered, on low heat, stirring occasionally till done (soft ends of okra will be considered as cooked). Serve hot.

- Select tender okra for better flavour.
- While cooking greens or any green vegetables, remove them from the pan as soon as they are cooked and cover the dish with a mesh instead of a lid to retain the green colour.

BEANS WITH BABY CORN
Beans aur Chotte Bhutte

INGREDIENTS

250 gm Haricot beans, cut diagonally to 1" pieces

12 Baby corn (*bhutta*), cut diagonally to 1" pieces

¼ tsp Sugar

1 tbsp / 15 ml Vegetable oil

2 tsp / 10 gm Black gram (*dhuli urad dal*), de-husked, soaked for 15 minutes

2 tsp / 10 gm Bengal gram (*chana dal*), de-husked, soaked for 15 minutes

½ tsp / 2½ gm Mustard seeds (*rai*)

¼ tsp Ginger (*adrak*) paste (see p. 191)

¼ tsp Garlic (*lasan*) paste (see p. 191)

2 Dry red chillies (*sookhi lal mirch*)

15 Curry leaves (*kadhi patta*)

Salt to taste

¼ tsp Black pepper (*kali mirch*)

2 tbsp / 30 gm Coconut (*nariyal*), grated

METHOD

- Boil 3½ cups water; add ¼ tsp sugar and cut beans; cook for 4 minutes. Drain.

- Boil 2½ cups water; add cut baby corn and cook for a minute. Drain.

- Heat 1 tbsp oil in a pan; add both the lentils and cook for 30 seconds. Add mustard seeds, ginger-garlic paste, dry red chillies, and curry leaves; mix well.

- Add beans, baby corn, salt to taste, and black pepper; cook for a minute. Add 1 tbsp coconut and mix.

- Remove and serve hot garnished with remaining coconut.

- This is a quick vegetable dish to prepare.
- Soaking helps the lentils to remain soft even after cooking.
- French beans can also be used instead of haricot beans.

Pure & Simple || MAIN COURSE || 94

BABY CORN AND CAPSICUM
Mazedaar Shimla Mirch aur Chhote Bhutte

Serves: 4-6

INGREDIENTS

30 Baby corn (*bhutta*), tender,
cut diagonally to 1" pieces
1 / 100 gm Capsicum (*Shimla
mirch*), medium-sized, cut
diagonally to 1" pieces
½ tbsp / 8 gm Corn flour
½ tbsp / 8 gm Gram flour
(*besan*)
¾ tsp / 4 gm Red chilli powder
(½ + ¼)
½ tsp / 2½ gm *Garam* masala
(¼ + ¼) (see p. 184)
¼ tsp Mango powder (*amchur*)
1 tbsp / 15 ml Milk
Vegetable oil for cooking and
deep-frying
2 tbsp / 30 gm Onion, chopped
1 tsp / 5 gm Garlic (*lasan*) paste
(see p. 191)
½ tsp / 2½ gm Green chilli
paste (see p. 191)
Salt and black pepper (*kali
mirch*) to taste
2 tsp / 10 ml Honey
½ cup / 50 gm Spring
onions (*hara pyaz*), chopped

METHOD

• Sprinkle ½ tbsp corn flour
and ½ tbsp gram flour over
the baby corn. Add ½ tsp red
chilli powder, ¼ tsp *garam
masala*, mango powder, and
milk; mix and leave aside for a
minute.

• Heat 1"-deep oil in a shallow
pan; deep-fry the baby corn
mixed with spices in medium-
hot oil for 2 minutes; keep
aside.

• Heat 1 tbsp oil in a pan for
30 seconds; add onion, garlic
and green chilli pastes; cook

for a minute. Add capsicum
and cook for 30 seconds.

• Add fried baby corn, salt to
taste, black pepper, honey, ¼
tsp red chilli powder, and ¼
tsp *garam* masala; mix well.
Add spring onions; mix.
Serve hot.

• Mix the baby corn with the vegetables just before serving for better
flavour and texture.

• This is a popular party dish.
• Cut corn should measure up to 2 cups and capsicum up to ¾ cup.

CORN A LA CILANTRO
Dhaniyawale Makai ke Dane

INGREDIENTS

1 cup / 100 gm Sweet corn (*makai*)
Vegetable oil for cooking
1 / 100 gm Onion, medium-sized, chopped
1 tsp / 5 gm Ginger (*adrak*), chopped
¼ tsp Garlic (*lasan*), chopped
¼ tsp Red chilli powder
2 tsp / 10 gm Coriander (*dhaniya*) powder
4 / 400 gm Tomatoes, medium-sized, 3 roasted and cut into cubes, 1 grated (see p. 186)
¼ tsp Sugar
Salt to taste
¼ tsp *Garam* masala (see p. 184)
2 tbsp Coriander (*dhaniya*) leaves, chopped

METHOD

- Heat 2 tsp oil in a pan for 30 seconds, add sweet corn and cook for 2 minutes on medium heat, stirring occasionally. Remove and keep aside.

- Heat 1 tbsp oil in the same pan for 30 seconds, add onion, ginger, and garlic; sauté till light pink. Add red chilli powder, and coriander powder, mix. Add cut and grated tomatoes and sugar, cook until semi-thick

- Add cooked corn, salt to taste, *garam* masala, and coriander leaves; cook for a minute on high heat. Serve hot.

- Fresh coriander leaves enhances the flavour in this dish.
- Sweet corn is also called American corn.

BEAN SPROUTS WITH CAPSICUM
Ankurit Moong aur Shimla Mirch

Serves: 4-6

INGREDIENTS

2 cups Bean sprouts
1 / 100 gm Capsicum (*Shimla mirch*), medium-sized, cut diagonally to 1" pieces
2 / 200 gm Tomatoes, medium-sized
½ cup / 100 gm Yoghurt (*dahi*)
2 tsp / 10 gm Gram flour (*besan*)
1 tbsp / 15 ml Vegetable oil
a pinch Asafoetida (*hing*)
½ tsp / 2½ gm Cumin (*jeera*) seeds
½ tsp / 2½ gm Ginger (*adrak*) paste (see p. 191)
¼ tsp Green chilli paste (see p. 191)
¼ tsp Turmeric (*haldi*) powder
$1/3$ tsp Red chilli powder
Salt to taste
¼ tsp *Garam* masala (see p. 184)
1 tbsp Coriander (*dhaniya*) leaves, chopped

METHOD

- Boil 3½ cups water; add bean sprouts and cook for 1½ minutes. Drain. Roast the tomatoes (see p. 186), peel and cut diagonally to 1" pieces.

- Mix yoghurt with 2 tsp gram flour to a smooth paste.

- Heat 1 tbsp oil in a pan; add asafoetida, cumin seeds, ginger and green chilli pastes. Add turmeric powder, red chilli powder, and yoghurt mixture; cook for 2 minutes.

- Add sprouts and salt to taste; cook until semi-thick.

- Add capsicum and tomatoes; cook for 2 minutes. Add *garam* masala and mix well. Serve hot garnished with coriander leaves.

- Cut capsicum should measure up to ½ cup and tomatoes up to 1 cup.
- Yoghurt and gram flour should be mixed properly, otherwise it may curdle.

- Sprouts are high in protein.
- Boiled sprouts mixed with tomato and salt can also be served for breakfast.

STUFFED GREEN CHILLIES
Bharwa Mirchi

INGREDIENTS

8 Light green chillies (*mirchi*)
1½ tbsp / 25 ml Mustard
(*sarson*) /Vegetable oil
a pinch Asafoetida (*hing*)
¼ tsp Cumin (*jeera*) seeds
¼ tsp Carom (*ajwain*) seeds
2 tsp / 10 gm Gram flour
(*besan*)

For the stuffing: mix and keep aside

4 / 300 gm Potatoes, medium-sized, boiled (see p. 183), peeled, grated
1½ tsp / 8 gm Fennel (*saunf*)
powder
½ tsp / 2½ gm Coriander
(*dhaniya*) powder
½ tsp / 2½ gm Mango powder
(*amchur*)
¼ tsp *Garam* masala
(see p. 184)
¼ tsp Red chilli powder
1 tbsp Coriander (*dhaniya*)
leaves, chopped
Salt to taste

METHOD

- Slit the green chillies vertically with a sharp knife, keeping the shape intact, and deseed.

- Stuff the chillies with the stuffing mixture tightly. Cut into 2 pieces.

- Heat 1½ tbsp oil in a pan for 30 seconds; add asafoetida, cumin seeds, carom seeds, and gram flour; cook for 10 seconds. Add stuffed chillies and cook on high heat for 2 minutes, stirring constantly. Serve hot.

- Stuffed green chillies are spicy in taste.
- The stuffing can also vary for example: grated masala cottage cheese (see p. 189) and *sookhi moong dal* (see p. 50) mixture can also be used.

BABY CARROTS WITH FENUGREEK LEAVES
Gajar Methi

INGREDIENTS

250 gm Baby carrots (*gajar*) peeled

2 cups / 100 gm Fenugreek, (*methi*) leaves, chopped, washed, dried over napkins

1½ tbsp / 25 ml Vegetable oil

a pinch Asafoetida (*hing*)

½ tsp / 2½ gm Cumin (*jeera*) seeds

Salt to taste

¼ tsp Sugar

½ tsp / 2½ gm Red chilli powder

1 tsp / 5 gm Coriander (*dhaniya*) powder

METHOD

- Heat 1½ tbsp oil in a pan; add asafoetida, cumin seeds, and carrots; sauté for a minute. Add ½ cup water, salt to taste, and sugar; cook covered on low heat till done.

- Add red chilli powder and coriander powder; cook for 30 seconds.

- Add fenugreek leaves and cook on high heat for a minute; toss frequently. Serve hot.

- Soft carrot ends will be taken as done.
- Both orange and red carrots can be used.

- Normally in India, red carrots are available during winter.
- Carrots are rich in vitamin A.

CABBAGE AND PEAS
Patta Gobi Mattar

INGREDIENTS

250 gm Cabbage (*bandh gobi*), cut into 1½" strips, rinsed, drained

¾ cup / 75 gm Green peas (*hara mattar*), shelled

1½ tbsp / 25 ml Vegetable oil

a pinch Asafoetida (*hing*)

½ tsp / 2½ gm Cumin (*jeera*) seeds

1 Green chilli, slit

¼ tsp Turmeric (*haldi*) powder

Salt to taste

¼ tsp *Garam* masala (see p. 184)

2 tbsp Coriander (*dhaniya*) leaves, chopped

METHOD

• Heat 1½ tbsp oil in a pan for 30 seconds; add asafoetida, cumin seeds, green chilli, and turmeric powder.

• Add green peas and cook for 30 seconds. Add cabbage and salt to taste; mix and cook covered on medium heat until soft.

• Add *garam* masala and coriander leaves; mix and serve hot.

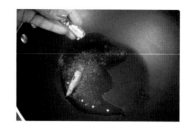

• This is a quick and healthy vegetable dish.
• Frozen peas can also be used.

GRAM FLOUR COATED ZUCCHINI
Besani Zucchini

INGREDIENTS

2 / 400 gm Zucchini, medium-sized, cut diagonally to 1" pieces
1½ tbsp / 25 ml Vegetable oil
¼ tsp Carom (*ajwain*) seeds
¼ tsp Cumin (*jeera*) seeds
1 tbsp / 15 gm Gram flour (*besan*)
¼ tsp Turmeric (*haldi*) powder
1 tsp / 5 gm Red chilli powder
2 tsp / 10 gm Coriander (*dhaniya*) powder
Salt to taste
¼ tsp Mango powder (*amchur*)
½ tsp / 2½ gm *Chaat* masala
2 tbsp Coriander (*dhaniya*) leaves, chopped

METHOD

- Heat 1½ tbsp oil in a pan for 30 seconds; add carom seeds, cumin seeds, gram flour, and turmeric powder. Cook for 10 seconds.

- Add cut zucchini, red chilli powder, coriander powder, and salt to taste; cook for 2 minutes on high heat, mixing frequently.

- Add mango powder, *chaat* masala, and coriander leaves; cook for a minute. Serve hot.

- Zucchini is also known as courgette.
- Zucchini has a shiny outer skin which is edible.
- Yellow zucchini is also available.

- Zucchini, cut into fingers and served with any dressing, makes a good salad.

HEALTHY LEAFY VEGETABLE
Hara Saag

INGREDIENTS

500 gm *Hara saag*, hard threads from stalks removed, chopped into fine pieces, washed, drained

2 tbsp / 30 ml Mustard (*sarson*) oil / Vegetable oil

¼ tsp Fenugreek seeds (*methi dana*)

2 tsp / 10 gm Ginger (*adrak*), chopped

1 tsp / 5 gm Green chillies, chopped

2 Dry red chillies (*sookhi lal mirch*)

Salt to taste

METHOD

• Heat 2 tbsp oil in a pan for 30 seconds; add fenugreek seeds, ginger, green chillies, dry red chillies, and *saag*; mix well. Cook, covered, for 2 minutes on high heat.

• Uncover, add salt to taste and cook open on high heat till the water evaporates, stirring occasionally. Serve hot.

• *Cholai* is a green leafy plant whose leaves and tender stems are cooked as *saag*. This *saag* is also available with a reddish tint.

• This *saag* is also called *cholai* saag or *dandi khere*.

CURRIED LOTUS STEMS
Sookhi Kamal Kakri

INGREDIENTS

250 gm Lotus stems (*kamal kakri*), peeled
3 tbsp / 45 ml Vegetable oil
2 / 150 gm Onions, medium-sized, peeled, grated
½ tsp / 2½ gm Ginger (*adrak*) paste (see p. 191)
¾ tsp / 4 gm Red chilli powder
½ tsp / 2½ gm Turmeric (*haldi*) powder
4 / 400 gm Tomatoes, medium-sized, liquidized (see p. 187)
Salt to taste
2 tbsp Coriander (*dhaniya*) leaves, chopped

METHOD

- Cut the lotus stems diagonally to ¼" pieces.

- Pressure cook the lotus stems with 2 cups water to one whistle and simmer for 2 minutes. Cool and drain.

- Heat 3 tbsp oil in a pan; add grated onion and fry until golden brown. Add ginger paste, red chilli powder, and turmeric powder; mix well.

- Add liquidized tomato and cook until semi-thick. Add lotus stems and salt to taste; cook, stirring occasionally, for 10 minutes or until dry.

- Serve hot garnished with coriander leaves.

- While buying lotus stems, select the white ones with closed ends as the open ended ones are muddy inside.

- Boiled lotus stem can also be used to prepare a spicy *chaat*.
- Lotus stem is considered a delicacy in Indian vegetarian cooking.

SWEET PUMPKIN
Meetha Kaddu

INGREDIENTS

250 gm Red pumpkin (*kaddu*), peeled, cut into ¾" cubes. Cut the peels into 1" pieces.
2 tbsp / 30 ml Vegetable oil
a pinch Asafoetida (*hing*)
½ tsp / 2½ gm Fenugreek seeds (*methi dana*)
2 tsp / 10 gm Ginger (*adrak*), chopped
1 tsp / 5 gm Green chillies, chopped
½ tsp / 2½ gm Turmeric (*haldi*) powder
½ tsp / 2½ gm Red chilli powder
Salt to taste
½ tsp / 2½ gm Mango powder (*amchur*)
1 tbsp / 15 gm Jaggery (*gur*), powdered
2 tbsp Coriander (*dhaniya*) leaves, chopped

METHOD

- Heat 2 tbsp oil in a pan for 30 seconds; add asafoetida and fenugreek seeds; sauté till brown. Add ginger, green chillies, turmeric powder; red chilli powder, and cut peels; cook for a minute. Add cut pumpkin and mix.

- Add salt to taste and ½ cup water; cook, covered, on high heat, stirring occasionally until the water evaporates.

- Uncover, add mango powder and jaggery; cook for a minute.

- Add coriander leaves; mix well. Serve hot.

- *Meetha kaddu* is a festival dish and is accompanied with *aloo tamatar rasedar* (see p. 109) and *urad dal kachori* (see p. 140).

STUFFED BITTER GOURD
Bharwa Karela

INGREDIENTS

250 gm Bitter gourd (*karela*), peeled, slit vertically with a sharp knife, keeping shape intact
Salt to apply inside bitter gourd
2 tbsp / 30 ml Mustard oil / Vegetable oil
a pinch Asafoetida (*hing*)
¼ Fenugreek seeds (*methi dana*)

For the stuffing: mix together
1½ tsp / 8 gm Fennel (*saunf*) powder
¾ tsp / 4 gm Coriander (*dhaniya*) powder
½ tsp / 2½ gm Red chilli powder
½ tsp / 2½ gm Turmeric (*haldi*) powder
½ tsp / 2½ gm Mango powder (*amchur*)
a pinch Asafoetida
Salt to taste

METHOD

- Apply one pinch salt inside each bitter gourd and leave aside for half an hour. Wash and squeeze the water out.

- Fill each bitter gourd with the stuffing masala evenly. Keep aside.

- Heat 1 tbsp mustard oil in a pressure cooker for 30 seconds; add asafoetida, fenugreek seeds, and stuffed bitter gourd; mix. Add ¼ cup water and cook to one whistle, on high heat. Reduce and simmer for 3 minutes and cool.

- Transfer bitter gourd to a non-stick pan; cook till the water evaporates. Add 1 tbsp oil and cook for 10 minutes on low heat, turning occasionally, until light golden brown. Serve hot.

- Tender, small bitter gourd tastes better because they are seedless.

- *Bharwa karela* can be kept in room temperature for 4 days after cooking, hence it can be a good travelling food item.

MIXED VEGETABLES WITH COTTAGE CHEESE
Sabz Paneer

INGREDIENTS

250 gm Cottage cheese
(*paneer*), cut into 1" fingers
(see p. 188)
8 French beans, cut diagonally to
1" pieces
2 / 100 gm Carrots (*gajar*),
medium-sized, cut diagonally to
1" pieces
1 / 100 gm Capsicum (*Shimla
mirch*), medium-sized, cut
diagonally to 1" pieces
2 tbsp / 30 ml Vegetable oil
Salt to taste
¼ tsp Sugar
$\frac{1}{8}$ tsp Turmeric (*haldi*) powder
½ tsp / 2½ gm Red chilli
powder
2 / 200 gm Tomatoes, medium-
sized, cut into cubes
1 tbsp / 15 gm Tomato sauce
¼ tsp *Garam* masala
(see p. 184)

METHOD

- Heat 1 tbsp oil in a pan for
  30 seconds; add cut French
  beans, carrots, capsicum, sugar,
  and salt to taste; cook,
  covered, on medium heat for
  2 minutes. Remove and keep
  aside.
- Heat 1 tbsp oil in the same
  pan; add turmeric powder, red
  chilli powder, and cut
  tomatoes; cook for a minute.
- Add tomato sauce, cottage
  cheese, and salt to taste; cook,
  covered, for a minute. Add
  cooked vegetables and *garam*
  masala; mix well and cook for
  a minute. Serve hot.

- *Sabz paneer* can be served any time with any meal.
- *Sabz paneer* is a healthy combination of proteins, calcium and fiber.

TOMATO FLAVOURED MIXED VEGETABLES
Milijuli Videshi Tarkariyan

INGREDIENTS

200 gm Broccoli, cut into 1½"
florets, blanched for a minute,
drained
150 gm Mushrooms (*khumb*),
cut into half, blanched for 20
seconds, drained
75 gm Red capsicum, deseeded,
cut into fingers
75 gm Yellow capsicum,
deseeded, cut into fingers
1½ tbsp / 25 ml Vegetable oil
2 / 100 gm Onions, medium-
sized, chopped
1 tsp / 5 gm Garlic (*lasan*) paste
(see p. 191)
½ tsp / 2½ gm Green chilli paste
(see p. 191)
2 / 200 gm Tomatoes, medium-
sized, chopped
½ tsp / 2½ gm *Chaat* masala
Salt to taste

For the tomato masala:

2 / 200 gm Tomatoes, medium-
sized, liquidized (see p. 187)
2 tsp / 10 ml Vegetable oil
¼ tsp Red chilli powder
1 tsp / 5 gm Coriander
(*dhaniya*) powder
1 tbsp / 15 gm Tomato sauce
¼ tsp *Garam* masala
(see p. 184)
Salt to taste

METHOD

- **For the tomato masala**, heat
  2 tsp oil in a pan for 30
  seconds; add red chilli powder,
  coriander powder, liquidized
  tomato, tomato sauce, *garam*
  masala, and salt to taste; cook
  on medium heat till the
  mixture thickens. Keep aside.

- Heat 1½ tbsp oil in a pan for
  30 seconds; add the onions
  and cook for a minute. Add
  garlic and green chilli pastes;
  cook for 10 seconds.

- Add red and yellow capsicum,
  tomatoes, broccoli, and
  mushrooms; cook for a
  minute on high heat.

- Add the tomato masala, *chaat*
  masala, and salt to taste; cook
  on high heat for a minute.
  Serve hot.

- Mixed vegetables taste best when mixed with tomato masala just
  before serving.

HOT POTATO CURRY
Aloo ka Jhol

Serves: 4

INGREDIENTS

4 / 400 gm Potatoes, medium-sized, boiled (see p. 183), peeled, broken into small pieces
1 tbsp / 15 ml Vegetable oil
a pinch Asafoetida (*hing*)
1 tsp / 5 gm Cumin (*jeera*) seeds
2 tsp / 10 gm Ginger (*adrak*), chopped
1 tsp / 5 gm Green chillies, chopped
½ tsp / 2½ gm Turmeric (*haldi*) powder
½ tsp / 2½ gm Red chilli powder
Salt to taste
½ tsp / 2½ gm Mango powder (*amchur*)
½ tsp / 2½ gm *Garam* masala (see p. 184)
2 tbsp Coriander (*dhaniya*) leaves, chopped

METHOD

- Heat 1 tbsp oil in a pan for 30 seconds; add asafoetida, cumin seeds, ginger, and green chillies; mix.

- Add turmeric powder, red chilli powder, potatoes, and 1½ cups water; mix well.

- Add salt to taste, mango powder, *garam* masala, and coriander leaves; bring to the boil. Reduce heat and simmer for 5 minutes. Serve hot.

- This potato dish is generally served with *meetha kaddu* (see p. 104), *sada paratha* (see p. 131) and *urad dal kachori* (see p. 140).

- Boiled potatoes are normally kept handy in Indian homes. They can be stored in the refrigerator for up to a week.

POTATOES IN TOMATO GRAVY
Aloo Tamatar Rasedar

Serves: 4-6

INGREDIENTS

4 / 400 gm Potatoes, medium-sized, peeled, cut into 1" cubes, immersed in water
3 / 300 gm Tomatoes, medium-sized, liquidized (see p. 187)
1½ tbsp / 25 ml Vegetable oil
a pinch Asafoetida (*hing*)
1 tsp / 5 gm Cumin (*jeera*) seeds
½ tsp / 2½ gm Turmeric (*haldi*) powder
¾ tsp / 4 gm Red chilli powder
1 tsp / 5 gm Ginger (*adrak*) paste (see p. 191)
½ tsp / 2½ gm Green chilli paste (see p. 191)
Salt to taste
2 tbsp Coriander (*dhaniya*) leaves, chopped
¼ tsp *Garam* masala (see p. 184)

METHOD

• Heat 1½ tbsp oil in a pressure cooker for 30 seconds; add asafoetida, cumin seeds, turmeric powder, red chilli powder, ginger paste, and green chilli paste; mix well. Add liquidized tomato and cook for 2 minutes.

• Add cut potatoes, 1¾ cups water, and salt to taste. Pressure cook to one whistle, simmer for 5 minutes and turn off the heat, cool.

• Uncover the lid, add coriander leaves and *garam* masala; bring to the boil, simmer for 2 minutes. Remove and serve hot.

• This preparation can also be prepared with boiled potatoes and cooked in a pan instead of a pressure cooker.

• Chopped ginger and chopped chillies can also be liquidized along with the tomatoes.

CURRIED COLOCASIA
Rasedar Arvi

INGREDIENTS

250 gm Colocasia (*arvi*), peeled, cut into small fingers
Vegetable oil for cooking and deep-frying
2 / 150 gm Onions, medium-sized, grated
½ tsp / 2½ gm Red chilli powder
½ tsp / 2½ gm Turmeric (*haldi*) powder
½ tsp / 2½ gm Coriander (*dhaniya*) powder
½ cup / 100 gm Yoghurt (*dahi*), 2-days-old, beaten (see p. 198)
Salt to taste
1 tbsp Coriander (*dhaniya*) leaves, chopped
2 tsp Mint (*pudina*), chopped
¼ tsp *Garam* masala (see p. 184)

METHOD

- Heat 1"-deep oil in a shallow pan; deep-fry colocasia fingers in medium-hot oil to light golden brown. Keep aside.

- Heat 2 tbsp oil in a pan for 30 seconds; add grated onion and fry till golden brown. Add red chilli powder, turmeric powder, and coriander powder; mix.

- Add beaten yoghurt and fry until oil separates.

- Add fried colocasia fingers, 1½ cups water, and salt to taste; bring to the boil and simmer for 5 minutes.

- Add coriander leaves, mint, and *garam* masala; mix. Serve hot.

- Beat yoghurt well, before adding to the gravy, to avoid separation.
- *Sada paratha* (see p. 131) is generally served with this dish.

CHICKPEAS WITH SPINACH GRAVY
Chana Palak

INGREDIENTS

1 cup / 175 gm Chickpeas (*kabuli chana*), soaked for 8 hours in plenty of water, drained
500 gm Spinach (*palak*), chopped, washed, drained in a colander
1 tbsp / 15 ml Vegetable oil
Salt to taste

Coarsely powdered:
½ tsp / 2½ gm Cumin (*jeera*) seeds
2 Cloves (*laung*)
4 Black peppercorns (*sabut kali mirch*)

For the garnishing:
1 tbsp / 15 ml Vegetable oil
1 / 100 gm Onion, large, cut into medium-sized cubes
2 tsp / 10 gm Ginger (*adrak*), chopped
2 / 200 Tomatoes, medium-sized, cut into cubes
Salt to taste

METHOD

- Pressure cook soaked chickpeas with 1¼ cups water and ¼ tsp salt to one whistle, simmer for 20 minutes, cool. Drain.

- Heat a pan for 30 seconds; add spinach and cook covered for 2 minutes. Remove and cool. Grind coarsely in a food processor. Keep aside.

- Heat 1 tbsp oil in a pan for 30 seconds; add coarsely powdered spices and cook for 10 seconds. Add boiled chickpeas and cook for a minute. Add puréed spinach and salt to taste; bring to the boil and simmer for 2 minutes. Transfer to a serving dish.

- **For the garnishing,** heat 1 tbsp oil in a pan; add onion and cook for a minute. Add ginger, tomatoes, and salt to taste. Cook for 30 seconds. Pour this mixture over the chickpeas evenly. Serve hot.

- The same recipe can be used for Corn and Spinach / Cottage Cheese and Spinach.

- Take 1 cup sweet corn for Corn and Spinach and 200 gm cottage cheese for Cottage Cheese and Spinach preparation.

SPICY CHICKPEAS
Chana Masala

INGREDIENTS

1 cup / 175 gm Chickpeas
(*kabuli chana*), soaked for 8
hours in plenty of water, drained
¼ tsp Baking soda
2 tbsp / 30 ml Vegetable oil
1 tsp / 5 gm Cumin (*jeera*) seeds
2 / 150 gm Onions, large,
chopped into small pieces
1 tsp / 5 gm Garlic (*lasan*) paste
(see p. 191)
1 tsp / 5 gm Red chilli powder
2 tsp / 10 gm Coriander
(*dhaniya*) powder
5 / 500 gm Tomatoes, medium-
sized, liquidized (see p. 187)
2 Green chillies, slit
1 tbsp / 15 gm Ginger (*adrak*),
julienned
2 tsp / 10 gm *Chana* masala
2 tbsp / 30 gm Pomegranate
seed (*anar dana*) powder
Salt to taste
2 tbsp Coriander (*dhaniya*)
leaves, chopped

Coarsely powdered:

4 Cloves (*laung*)
2 Black cardamom (*badi elaichi*)
2 Green cardamom (*choti
elaichi*)
1" Cinnamon (*dalchini*) stick

METHOD

- Pressure cook chickpeas with
  baking soda and 2½ cups
  water (see p. 193).

- Heat 2 tbsp oil in a pan for
  30 seconds; add cumin seeds,
  onions, and garlic paste; fry till
  light brown. Add coarsely
  powdered spices and mix.

- Add red chilli powder,
  coriander powder, and
  liquidized tomato; fry till oil
  separates.

- Add boiled chickpeas along
  with water, green chillies,
  ginger, *chana* masala,
  pomegranate seed powder,
  and salt to taste. Bring the
  mixture to the boil and
  simmer for 10 minutes.

- Add coriander leaves.
  Serve hot.

- Pomegranate seed powder is available in any Indian grocery store. It is
  basically dried and powdered pomegranate seeds. The colour of the
  dish changes to dark brown after adding this powder.

- This dish can be garnished with cut tomatoes, onions, ginger, and chillies.
- Chickpeas is a popular Indian dish usually accompanied with *bhatura*
  (see p. 141).

TANGY BOTTLE GOURD
Lauki Tamatardar

INGREDIENTS

500 gm Bottle gourd (*lauki*), peeled, cut into 1" cubes
2 / 200 gm Tomatoes, medium-sized, grated (see p. 186)
1 tsp / 5 gm Clarified butter (*ghee*)
a pinch Asafoetida (*hing*)
½ tsp / 2½ gm Cumin (*jeera*) seeds
2 tsp / 10 gm Ginger (*adrak*), chopped
½ tsp / 2½ gm Turmeric (*haldi*) powder
Salt to taste
2 tbsp Coriander (*dhaniya*) leaves, chopped

METHOD

- Heat 1 tsp clarified butter in a pressure cooker for 30 seconds; add asafoetida, cumin seeds, ginger, turmeric powder, and bottle gourd; mix well.

- Add 1 cup water and salt to taste and pressure cook to one whistle. Reduce heat and simmer for 5 minutes. Cool.

- Uncover, add grated tomato and cook till semi-thick.

- Add coriander leaves and mix. Serve hot.

- Bottle gourd is a light vegetable, generally recommended to patients and the calorie-conscious.
- This dish can also be prepared without tomatoes.

BOTTLE GOURD DUMPLINGS IN TOMATO GRAVY
Lauki Kofta

INGREDIENTS

For the koftas:

300 gm Bottle gourd (*lauki*), peeled, grated
a pinch Asafoetida (*hing*)
4 tbsp / 60 gm Gram flour (*besan*)
¼ tsp Salt
1 tbsp Coriander (*dhaniya*) leaves, chopped
Vegetable oil for deep-frying

For the gravy:

1½ tbsp / 25 ml Vegetable oil
a pinch Asafoetida
1 tsp / 5 gm Cumin (*jeera*) seeds
½ tsp / 2½ gm Turmeric (*haldi*) powder
¾ tsp / 4 gm Red chilli powder
1 tsp / 5 gm Ginger (*adrak*), chopped
4 / 400 gm Tomatoes, medium-sized, liquidized (see p. 187)
2 tbsp / 30 gm Yoghurt (*dahi*), beaten (see p. 198)
Salt to taste
¼ tsp *Garam* masala (see p. 184)
1 tbsp Coriander leaves, chopped

METHOD

- **For the koftas,** mix the grated bottle gourd with asafoetida, gram flour, salt, and coriander leaves. Divide the mixture equally into 20 balls.

- Heat 1"-deep oil in a shallow pan; deep-fry, 10 balls at a time, in medium-hot oil, until light golden brown. Keep aside. Repeat till all are fried.

- **For the gravy,** heat 1½ tbsp oil in a pan for 30 seconds; add asafoetida, cumin seeds, turmeric powder, red chilli powder, and ginger; mix. Add liquidized tomato and fry until the oil separates. Add beaten yoghurt and cook for a minute.

- Add the fried balls, 3 cups water, and salt to taste. Bring the mixture to the boil reduce heat and simmer for 5 minutes. Add *garam* masala and coriander leaves; mix well. Serve hot.

- Don't leave the bottle gourd mixed with gram flour and salt for a long time as this leaves water and hence it becomes difficult to shape into balls.

- Grated bottle gourd turns brown if left unused for a long time. So grate just before preparing.

LEMON FLAVOURED RIDGE GOURD
Rasedar Turai

Serves: 4

INGREDIENTS

1 kg Ridge gourd (*turai*), peeled, cut into ½" semi-circles
1 tsp / 5 gm Clarified butter (*ghee*)
a pinch Asafoetida (*hing*)
½ tsp / 2½ gm Cumin (*jeera*) seeds
⅛ tsp Turmeric (*haldi*) powder
Salt to taste
2 tbsp Coriander (*dhaniya*) leaves, chopped
½ tsp / 2½ ml Lemon (*nimbu*) juice

METHOD

- Heat 1 tsp clarified butter in a pressure cooker for 30 seconds; add asafoetida, cumin seeds, turmeric powder, ridge gourd, and salt to taste; mix. Pressure cook to one whistle. Cool.

- Uncover pressure cooker lid and bring the mixture to the boil.

- Add coriander leaves and lemon juice; mix well and turn off the heat. Serve hot.

- Ridge gourd can also be prepared in a pan on low heat until soft.
- Ridge gourd is easy-to-digest and served as a part of a light Indian meal.

BLACK-EYED BEANS IN GRAVY
Lobhia Taridar

INGREDIENTS

1 cup / 175 gm White black-eyed beans (*lobhia*), soaked for 4 hours in plenty of water, drained

Salt to taste

½ tsp / 2½ gm Turmeric (*haldi*) powder (¼ + ¼)

1 tbsp / 15 ml Vegetable oil

a pinch Asafoetida (*hing*)

⅓ tsp Cumin (*jeera*) seeds

½ tsp / 2½ gm Red chilli powder

3 / 300 Tomatoes, medium-sized, liquidized (see p. 187)

1 tsp / 5 gm Ginger (*adrak*) paste (see p. 191)

¼ tsp Green chilli paste (see p. 191)

Salt to taste

¼ tsp *Garam* masala (see p. 184)

2 tbsp Coriander (*dhaniya*) leaves, chopped

METHOD

• Pressure cook the black-eyed beans with 2 cups water, salt to taste, and ¼ tsp turmeric powder to one whistle; simmer for 5 minutes and cool (see p. 193).

• Heat 1 tbsp oil in a pan for 30 seconds; add asafoetida, cumin seeds, red chilli powder, ¼ tsp turmeric powder, liquidized tomato, ginger paste, and green chilli paste; fry till oil separates. Add boiled black-eyed beans along with the water.

• Add salt to taste and bring to the boil. Reduce heat and simmer on low heat till semi-thick. Add *garam* masala and coriander leaves. Serve hot.

• Pressure cooked black-eyed beans can be used in salads, after discarding the water.

COTTAGE CHEESE WITH PEAS IN GRAVY
Mattar Paneer

INGREDIENTS

250 gm Cottage cheese
(*paneer*), cut into slices
(see p. 188)
2 cups / 200 gm Green peas
(*hara mattar*), boiled
4 tbsp / 60 ml Vegetable oil
2 Bay leaves (*tej patta*)
2 / 150 gm Onions, medium-
sized, grated
1 tsp / 5 gm Ginger (*adrak*) paste
(see p. 191)
¾ tsp / 4 gm Red chilli powder
¾ tsp / 4 gm Turmeric (*haldi*)
powder
3 / 300 gm Tomatoes, medium-
sized, liquidized (see p. 187)
2 tbsp / 30 gm Yoghurt (*dahi*),
beaten (see p. 198)
2 tbsp / 30 gm Cream
a pinch Sugar
¼ tsp *Garam* masala
(see p. 184)
1 tbsp Coriander (*dhaniya*)
leaves, chopped

METHOD

• Heat 1 tbsp oil in a non-stick pan for 30 seconds; add cottage
  cheese and fry, on medium heat, on both sides until light brown
  (see p. 189). Remove, cool and cut into 1" cubes. Keep aside.

• Heat 3 tbsp oil in a pan for 30 seconds; add bay leaves, grated
  onion, and ginger paste; fry till light golden brown, stirring
  occasionally. Add red chilli powder and turmeric powder; mix
  well. Add liquidized tomato and fry until the oil separates. Add
  beaten yoghurt and fry till oil separates.

• Add cream, green peas, and cottage cheese; cook for a minute.

• Add 1½ cups water, salt to taste, and sugar. Bring to the boil and
  simmer for 5 minutes. Add *garam* masala and coriander leaves;
  mix. Serve hot.

• Cream adds a better texture and taste to this gravy. Calorie watchers   • This onion-tomato gravy can be used for other gravy dishes as well.
  can avoid cream.

LENTIL DUMPLINGS WITH FENUGREEK AND PEAS
Methi Magori Mattar

Serves: 4-6

INGREDIENTS

1 cup / 100 gm Dry lentil dumplings (*magori*)
1½ cups / 75 gm Fenugreek (*methi*) leaves, chopped, cooked (see p. 196)
¾ cup / 75 gm Green peas (*hara mattar*), boiled
Vegetable oil for cooking and deep-frying
Salt to taste
a pinch Asafoetida (*hing*)
½ tsp / 2½ gm Cumin (*jeera*) seeds
½ tsp / 2½ gm Ginger (*adrak*) paste (see p. 191)
¼ tsp Green chilli paste (see p. 191)
½ tsp / 2½ gm Red chilli powder
½ tsp / 2½ gm Turmeric (*haldi*) powder
3 / 300 gm Tomatoes, medium-sized, liquidized (see p. 187)
¼ tsp *Garam* masala (see p. 184)
2 tbsp Coriander (*dhaniya*) leaves, chopped

METHOD

- Heat ½"-deep oil in a shallow pan; deep-fry the lentil dumplings in medium-hot oil until light golden (see p. 185) brown. Keep aside.

- Heat 2 tsp oil in a pan for 30 seconds; add boiled peas and cook for minute. Add salt to taste. Keep aside.

- Heat 2 tsp oil in a pressure cooker; add fried lentil dumplings, 2 cups water, and salt to taste. Cook till one whistle, then simmer for 5 minutes, cool. Keep aside.

- Heat 1 tbsp oil in a pan for 30 seconds; add asafoetida, cumin seeds, ginger paste, green chilli paste, red chilli powder, and turmeric powder; mix. Add liquidized tomato and bring to the boil. Cook for 2 minutes, on medium heat. Add fenugreek leaves and cook for a minute.

- Add pressure cooked dumplings along with water and bring to the boil, simmer for 5 minutes. Add *garam* masala and mix.

- Add cooked peas and coriander leaves; cook for 2 minutes. Serve hot.

- This dish is relished with *sada* roti (see p. 137).

- Fenugreek leaves add a delicate bitter flavour to the dish..

BITTER SWEET CREAMY PEAS
Methi Malai Mattar

INGREDIENTS

1 cup / 100 gm Green peas
(*hara mattar*), boiled
1½ cups / 75 gm Fenugreek
(*methi*) leaves, chopped
Salt to taste
1½ tbsp / 25 ml Vegetable oil
1 / 100 gm Onion, large, grated
1 tsp / 5 gm Ginger (*adrak*) paste
(see p. 191).
½ tsp / 2½ gm Garlic (*lasan*)
paste (see p. 191)
½ tsp / 2½ gm Red chilli
powder
½ tsp / 2½ gm Coriander
powder
2 / 200 gm Tomatoes, medium-
sized, grated (see p. 186)
2 tsp / 10 gm White butter
1 tbsp / 15 ml Cream
2 tbsp / 30 ml Milk
¼ tsp Sugar
¼ tsp *Garam* masala
(see p. 184)

METHOD

• Add ½ tsp salt to fenugreek leaves, mix and leave aside for 5
minutes. Squeeze and keep aside.

• Heat 1½ tbsp oil in a pan for 30 seconds, add grated onion,
ginger and garlic pastes; cook on medium heat until light pink. Add
squeezed fenugreek leaves and cook for minute. Add red chilli
powder and coriander powder, mix well.

• Add grated tomato and cook for a minute.

• Add boiled peas, white butter, cream, milk, salt to taste, and sugar,
bring to the boil and simmer for 2 minutes. Add *garam* masala
and mix well. Serve hot.

• The process of squeezing the fenugreek leaves to remove the excess
water, after adding salt, reduces the bitterness.

RICE & BREADS

PEAS AND CARROT PILAF
Gajar Mattar Pulao

Serves: 4

INGREDIENTS

1 cup / 175 gm Basmati rice
2 / 100 gm Carrots (*gajar*), medium-sized, chopped
½ cup / 50 gm Green peas (*hara mattar*)
1 tbsp / 15 gm Clarified butter (*ghee*)
2 Cloves (*laung*)
½ tsp / 2½ gm Cumin (*jeera*) seeds
2 cups / 400 ml Water
Salt to taste

METHOD

- Wash and soak the rice in plenty of water for 20 minutes. Drain.

- Heat 1 tbsp clarified butter in a pan for 30 seconds; add cloves, cumin seeds, peas, and carrots. Cook for a minute on medium heat.

- Add soaked rice, 2 cups water, and salt to taste; bring to the boil and cook, covered, on low heat, till water evaporates or until rice is done. Serve hot.

- To get good textured rice, it is advised to cook it, covered, on low heat, after one boil.
- Stirring rice constantly while cooking breaks the grains.

- Any pilaf accompanied by flavoured yoghurt, of your choice, is a complete meal.

CORN PILAF
Bhutte ka Pulao

INGREDIENTS

1 cup / 175 gm Basmati rice
1 cup / 100 gm Corn (*bhutta*)
1 tbsp / 15 gm Clarified butter (*ghee*)
¼ tsp Black pepper (*kali mirch*)
1" Cinnamon (*dalchini*) stick
½ cup Spring onions (*hara pyaz*), chopped
½ cup / 50 gm Capsicum (*Shimla mirch*), chopped
2 cups / 400 ml Water
Salt to taste

METHOD

- Wash and soak the rice in plenty of water for 30 minutes. Drain.

- Heat 1 tbsp clarified butter in a pan for 30 seconds: add black pepper and cinnamon stick.

- Add chopped spring onions, capsicum, and corn; cook for 30 seconds.

- Add soaked rice, 2 cups water, and salt to taste; bring to the boil. Cover and cook on low heat till water evaporates or until rice is done. Serve hot.

- The water quantity used to cook the rice should always be double the quantity of raw rice.

CUMIN PILAF
Jeera Pulao

INGREDIENTS

1 cup / 175 gm Basmati rice
1 tbsp / 15 gm Clarified butter (*ghee*)
2 Bay leaves (*tej patta*)
2 Black cardamom (*badi elaichi*)
4 Cloves (*laung*)
1" Cinnamon (*dalchini*) stick
1 tsp / 5 gm Cumin (*jeera*) seeds
2 cups / 400 ml Water
Salt to taste
1 tbsp Coriander (*dhaniya*) leaves, chopped

METHOD

• Wash and soak the rice in plenty of water for 30 minutes. Drain

• Heat 1 tbsp clarified butter in a pan for 30 seconds; add bay leaves, black cardamom, cloves, cinnamon stick, and cumin seeds; stir-fry.

• Add soaked rice and cook for 10 seconds.

• Add 2 cups water and salt to taste; bring to the boil. Cover and cook on low heat till the water evaporates or until rice is done.

• Serve hot garnished with coriander leaves.

• Cumin pilaf is very safe to make as it goes with any combination of lentil and gravy dish.

• Basmati rice has a unique aroma and flavour, but any good quality long-grain rice can also be used.

MIXED VEGETABLE LENTIL RICE
Sabzion ki Kichadi

Serves: 2-4

INGREDIENTS
½ cup / 90 gm Rice, small grain
½ cup / 75 gm Split green gram
(*dhuli moong dal*)
¾ cup / 75 gm Green peas
(*hara mattar*)
¾ cup / 100 gm Carrots (*gajar*),
chopped
¾ cup / 100 gm Cauliflower
(*phool gobi*) florets
1 cup / 150 gm Potatoes, cubed
½ tsp / 2½ gm Turmeric (*haldi*)
powder
½ tsp / 2½ gm Salt
2 tbsp Coriander (*dhaniya*)
leaves, chopped
For the tempering:
1 tbsp / 15 gm Clarified butter
(*ghee*)
a pinch Asafoetida (*hing*)
1 tsp / 5 gm Cumin (*jeera*)
seeds
2 Cloves (*laung*)
2 Black cardamom (*badi elaichi*)
½" Cinnamon (*dalchini*) stick

METHOD
• Wash and soak the rice and green gram together in plenty of
  water for 30 minutes. Drain.

• Pressure cook the rice and green gram with cut vegetables,
  3 cups water, salt, and turmeric powder to one whistle. Keep
  aside to cool.

• Uncover the pressure cooker lid and bring the mixture to the
  boil. Add coriander leaves. Season with the tempering.

• **For the tempering,** heat 1 tbsp clarified butter in a pan for 30
  seconds; add asafoetida, cumin seeds, cloves, black cardamom, and
  cinnamon stick. Top it evenly over the rice mixture. Serve hot.

• *Kichadi* is always served with yoghurt, pickle and *papad*.
• *Kichadi* can also be prepared without vegetables.

• Use all forms of green gram except the whole (*sabut*) lentil.
• *Kichadi* is a complete one-meal dish.

FENUGREEK FLAVOURED COTTAGE CHEESE PILAF
Methi Paneer Pulao

INGREDIENTS

1 cup / 175 gm Basmati rice
1 cup / 50 gm Fenugreek
(*methi*) leaves, chopped
200 gm Cottage cheese
(*paneer*), cut into slices
(see p. 188)
2 tsp / 10 ml Vegetable oil
1½ tbsp / 25 gm Clarified
butter (*ghee*)
2 / 150 gm Onions, medium-
sized, cut into cubes
½ cup Coriander (*dhaniya*)
leaves, chopped
2 / 150 gm Tomatoes, medium-
sized, cut into 8 pieces, liquidized
(see p. 187)
2 cups / 400 ml Water
Salt to taste

METHOD

- Wash and soak the rice in plenty of water for 30 minutes. Drain.

- Heat 2 tsp oil in a non-stick pan for 30 seconds; sauté the cottage cheese till light golden brown on both sides. (see p. 189). Remove and cut into 1" cubes. Keep aside.

- Heat 1 tbsp clarified butter in a pan for 30 seconds; add chopped onions and fry till light brown. Add fenugreek leaves and coriander leaves; cook for a minute.

- Add liquidized tomato and cook for a minute.

- Add soaked rice, 2 cups water, and salt to taste; bring to the boil. Cover and cook on low heat.

- When the rice is half-cooked, add cottage cheese and cook till the rice is done. Serve hot.

- *Pulao* is a rice dish containing spices to which vegetables may or may not be added.

MIXED VEGETABLE PILAF
Sabz Pulao

INGREDIENTS

1 cup / 175 gm Basmati rice
2 / 150 gm Potatoes, medium-sized, cut into cubes
1 cup / 100 gm Cauliflower (*phool gobi*) florets
1 cup / 100 gm Green peas (*hara mattar*)
1 tbsp / 15 gm Clarified butter (*ghee*)
1 tsp / 5 gm Cumin (*jeera*) seeds
½ tsp / 2½ gm Turmeric (*haldi*) powder
2 cups / 400 ml Water
1½ tsp / 8 gm Salt

METHOD

• Wash and soak the rice in plenty of water for 30 minutes. Drain.

• Heat 1 tbsp clarified butter in a pan for 30 seconds; add cumin seeds and turmeric powder. Add potatoes, cauliflower, and peas; mix well. Cook for a minute on medium heat. Add soaked rice and mix.

• Add 2 cups water and salt; bring to the boil. Cover and cook on low heat till the water evaporates or until rice is done.

• Soft firm texture of rice checked with index finger is considered to be done.
• Soaking helps the rice to cook properly and evenly.

• Always cook rice dishes in a flat pan to get better texture.
• This *pulao* is usually prepared in winter as peas and cauliflower are in abundance.

SPICY LENTIL RICE
Dal Biryani

INGREDIENTS

1 cup / 175 gm Basmati rice
¼ cup / 40 gm Yellow lentil (*arhar dal*)
Vegetable oil for deep-frying
2 / 150 gm Potatoes, medium-sized, cut into cubes
2 / 150 gm Onions, medium-sized, cut into flakes
1 tbsp / 15 gm Clarified butter (*ghee*)
2 cups / 400 ml Water
Salt to taste
¼ tsp *Garam* masala (see p. 184)
1 tbsp Coriander (*dhaniya*) leaves, chopped

For seasoning 1:
½ tsp / 2½ gm Cumin (*jeera*) seeds
½ tsp / 2½ gm Ginger (*adrak*) paste (see p. 191)
½ tsp / 2½ gm Garlic (*lasan*) paste (see p. 191)
½ tsp / 2½ gm Green chilli paste (see p. 191)

For seasoning 2:
½" Cinnamon (*dalchini*) stick
2 Black cardamom (*badi elaichi*)
¼ tsp Turmeric (*haldi*) powder

METHOD

- Wash and soak the rice and yellow lentil separately in plenty of water for 30 minutes. Drain.

- Deep-fry the potatoes in medium-hot oil till light golden brown. Remove and keep aside.

- Deep-fry the onions in hot oil till light golden brown. Remove and keep aside.

- Heat 1 tbsp clarified butter in a pan for 30 seconds; add all the ingredients of seasoning 1 and mix well. Add seasoning 2 and mix again.

- Add soaked rice and lentil; cook for 30 seconds. Add 2 cups water and salt to taste; bring the mixture to the boil. Cover and cook on low heat, till water evaporates or until rice is done.

- Add fried potatoes and onions, and *garam* masala; mix. Serve hot garnished with coriander leaves.

- This dish is a complete meal in itself with a combination of rice and lentil together.
- *Dal Biryani* can also be accompanied with plain yoghurt.

TOMATO RICE
Tamatar ke Chawal

Serves: 2-4

INGREDIENTS

1 cup / 175 gm Basmati rice
4 / 400 gm Tomatoes, medium-sized, cut into 8 pieces, liquidized (see p. 187)
1 tbsp / 15 gm Clarified butter (ghee)
¼ tsp Mustard seeds (rai)
¼ tsp Cumin (jeera) seeds
15 Curry leaves (kadhi patta)
2 tsp / 10 gm Bengal gram (chana dal), de-husked, split
2 tsp / 10 gm Black gram (dhuli urad dal), de-husked, split
2 / 150 gm Onions, medium-sized, chopped into medium-sized cubes
¼ tsp Turmeric (haldi) powder
¼ Red chilli powder
Salt to taste
2 tbsp Coriander (dhaniya) leaves, chopped
2 tbsp Peanuts (moongphalli), skinned

METHOD

• Wash and soak the rice in plenty of water for 30 minutes. Drain. Boil the rice (see p. 190) in water. Drain and keep aside.

• Heat 1 tbsp clarified butter in a pan for 30 seconds; add mustard seeds, cumin seeds, curry leaves, Bengal gram, and black gram; cook till light pink in colour.

• Add the onions and cook till light brown. Add turmeric and red chilli powders; mix. Add liquidized tomato and cook till thick.

• Add boiled rice and mix lightly.

• Add salt to taste, coriander leaves, and peanuts; cook on low heat for 5 minutes, stirring occasionally. Serve hot.

• Leftover rice can also be used to prepare this dish

• Tomato rice has a nutty flavour.

HEALTHY VEGETABLE PILAF
Hariyali Pulao

Serves: 4-6

INGREDIENTS

1 cup / 175 gm Basmati Rice
1 cup / 75 gm Broccoli florets
1½ cups / 150 gm Zucchini, cut diagonally
1½ cups / 75 gm Spinach (*palak*), chopped
1 tbsp / 15 gm Clarified butter (*ghee*)
¼ tsp Black pepper (*kali mirch*)
2 cups / 400 ml Water
Salt to taste

METHOD

- Wash and soak the rice in plenty of water for 20 minutes, Drain.

- Heat 1 tbsp clarified butter in a pan for 30 seconds, add black pepper and spinach, cook for 30 seconds. Add broccoli and zucchini, and cook for 30 seconds more.

- Add soaked rice, 2 cups water, and salt to taste; bring to the boil. Cook, covered, on low heat till done. Serve hot.

- *Hariyali pulao* is enjoyed by everyone because of its delicate flavouring and the natural taste of vegetables.

SHALLOW FRIED PLAIN BREAD
Sada Paratha

Serves: 4-6

INGREDIENTS

2 cups / 250 gm Wholewheat
flour (*atta*)
½ tsp / 2½ gm Salt
¾ cup / 150 ml Water to make
the dough
Vegetable oil for shallow-frying

METHOD

- Sieve the wholewheat flour with salt. Knead to make a normal dough with water (see p. 190). Keep covered for 10 minutes.

- Divide the dough into 12 equal balls. Take a ball, dust and roll with a rolling pin slightly, apply ½ tsp oil, sprinkle wholewheat flour and fold into a triangle. Dust and roll into 5½" triangle.

- Shallow-fry each *paratha* on a heated griddle (*tawa*) with 2 tsp oil until light golden brown on both sides. Serve hot.

- Fold the *paratha* first into a semi-circle and then fold the semi-circle into a triangle.
- Fresh *paratha* can be fried soft or crisp as per individual taste.

- For storing *paratha*, fry lightly so that it remains soft.

INDIAN BREAD STUFFED WITH POTATOES
Aloo Paratha

INGREDIENTS

2 cups / 250 gm Wholewheat flour (*atta*)

½ tsp / 2½ gm Salt

½ tbsp / 8 gm Clarified butter (*ghee*), melted

¾ cup / 150 ml Water to prepare dough

Vegetable oil for shallow-frying

For the filling:

4 / 300 gm Potatoes, medium-sized, boiled (see p. 183), peeled, mashed

1 tsp / 5 gm Fennel (*saunf*) powder

1 tsp / 5 gm Green chillies, chopped

1 tbsp Coriander (*dhaniya*) leaves, chopped

¼ tsp Mango powder (*amchur*)

Salt to taste

METHOD

- Sieve the wholewheat flour with salt. Add clarified butter and knead to make a normal dough with water. Keep covered for 10 minutes.

- **For the filling**, mix the mashed potato with fennel powder, green chillies, coriander leaves, mango powder, and salt to taste. Keep aside.

- Divide the dough and the filling each into 8 portions. Roll a portion of the dough slightly, stuff with 1 tbsp filling and fold to seal the filling inside. Dust with flour and roll with a rolling pin into a 6" disc.

- Add ½ tsp oil on a heated griddle (*tawa*) and shallow-fry each disc with 2 tbsp oil until light golden brown on both sides. Serve hot.

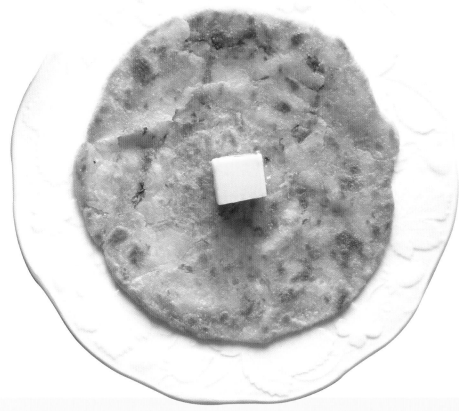

- Stuffed *paratha* is a quick and popular meal.
- Variations can be made by changing the base of the filling to grated cauliflower, grated cottage cheese, or chopped onions.
- It can be served with yoghurt, pickle, and butter.
- For calorie watchers reduce oil while shallow-frying and omit butter while serving.

Pure & Simple || RICE & BREADS || 132

DOUBLE-DECKER INDIAN BREAD
Tiranga Paratha

INGREDIENTS

2 cups / 250 gm Wholewheat flour (*atta*)
½ tsp / 2½ gm Salt
1 tbsp / 15 gm Clarified butter (*ghee*), melted
¾ cup / 150 ml Water to make the dough
Vegetable oil for cooking

For filling 1:
200 gm Cottage cheese (*paneer*), grated (see p. 188)
½ tsp / 2½ gm Black pepper (*kali mirch*)
2 tbsp Coriander (*dhaniya*) leaves, chopped
Salt to taste

For filling 2:
½ tsp / 2½ gm Green chilli paste (see p. 191)
200 gm Green peas (*hara mattar*), boiled, mashed coarsely
1 tbsp / 15 ml Vegetable oil
½ tsp / 2½ gm Mango powder (*amchur*)
¼ tsp *Garam* masala (see p. 184)
¼ tsp Salt
2 tbsp Coriander leaves, chopped

METHOD

• Sieve the wholewheat flour with salt. Add melted clarified butter and knead to make a normal dough with water. Keep covered for 15 minutes.

• **For filling 1**, mix the grated cottage cheese with black pepper, coriander leaves, and salt to taste. Keep aside.

• **For filling 2**, heat 1 tbsp oil in a pan for 30 seconds; add green chilli paste and peas, cook for a minute. Add mango powder, *garam* masala, salt to taste, and coriander leaves; cook on low heat for 2 minutes, stirring occasionally. Remove and keep aside.

• Divide the dough into 21 balls.

• Take three balls, roll them slightly and place a portion of filling 1 on one round, cover with the second round and place a portion of filling 2 on the second round and cover with the third round.

• Press the edges, dust with flour and roll into a 7" disc. Shallow-fry each disc on a heated griddle (*tawa*) with 2 tbsp oil till light golden brown. Remove and serve hot.

• Approximately ¾ cup water is required to make the dough.
• *Tiranga paratha* can be served with plain yoghurt or *raita*.

• *Tiranga paratha* makes an ideal Sunday breakfast.

FLAKY MINT BREAD
Lachchedar Paratha

Serves: 2-4

INGREDIENTS

1 cup / 125 gm Wholewheat flour (*atta*)
1 cup / 125 gm All purpose flour (*maida*)
½ tsp / 2½ gm Salt
½ cup / 100 ml Milk
¼ cup / 50 ml Water (approx.) to make the dough
Clarified butter (*ghee*) and Mint (*pudina*) powder (see p. 11) to apply inside
Vegetable oil / Clarified butter for cooking

METHOD

• Sieve both the flours with salt. Add milk and knead to make a soft dough with water. Keep covered for 15 minutes.

• Divide the dough equally into 5 balls; flatten each ball with a rolling pin, apply 2 tsp clarified butter, sprinkle ¼ tsp mint powder, and ½ tsp wholewheat flour. Fold one end to another forming 1" pleats like a cylinder.

• Fold the cylinder to form a flat ball (*peda*). Dust and roll with a rolling pin into a 6" disc.

• Shallow-fry each *paratha* on a heated griddle (*tawa*) with 2 tbsp oil till light golden brown.

• Remove and crush along with a napkin. Serve hot.

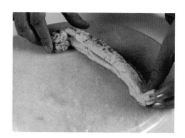

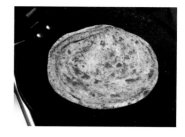

• By making a soft dough and sprinkling wholewheat flour helps the layers to open easily.

• *Lachchedar paratha* can also be roasted directly on heat like *sada* roti (see p. 137).

CALABASH BREAD
Lauki Paratha

INGREDIENTS

1½ cups / 175 gm Wholewheat flour (*atta*)
½ cup / 50 gm Gram flour (*besan*)
¾ tsp / 4 gm Salt
2 tbsp / 30 gm Yoghurt (*dahi*)
300 gm Bottle gourd (*lauki*), grated
½ tsp / 2½ gm Carom (*ajwain*) seeds
2 tbsp Coriander (*dhaniya*) leaves, chopped
½ tsp / 2½ gm Red chilli powder
¼ tsp Turmeric (*haldi*) powder
Vegetable oil for cooking

METHOD

- Sieve the wholewheat flour and gram flour with salt. Add yoghurt, grated bottle gourd, carom seeds, coriander leaves, red chilli powder, and turmeric powder.

- Knead to make a normal dough with water. Keep aside covered for 5 minutes.

- Divide the dough into 12 equal balls. Dust and roll each ball slightly with a rolling pin, apply ¼ tsp oil and fold into a triangle (see p. 131).

- Dust and roll again to 4" triangle.

- Shallow-fry each *paratha* on a heated griddle (*tawa*) with 1 tbsp oil until light golden brown. Serve hot.

- Bottle gourd leaves water if left unused for a longer time. Always prepare fresh dough as it is easier to roll.

SPICY INDIAN BREAD
Masala Paratha

INGREDIENTS

2 cups / 250 gm Wholewheat flour (*atta*)
½ tsp / 2½ gm Salt
2 tbsp / 30 gm Yoghurt (*dahi*)
¾ cup / 150 ml Water to make the dough
Vegetable oil for applying inside and for shallow-frying
4 tbsp Coriander (*dhaniya*) leaves, chopped

For the masala to apply inside: mix together

¼ tsp Asafoetida (*hing*)
¾ tsp / 4 gm Salt
2 tsp / 10 gm Red chilli powder
½ tsp / 2½ gm Carom (*ajwain*) seeds
1 tsp / 5 gm Cumin (*jeera*) seeds

METHOD

- Sieve wholewheat flour with salt. Add yoghurt and knead to make a normal dough with water. Keep covered for 10 minutes.

- Divide the dough into 8 equal balls, dust each ball and roll into 6" diameter. Apply 2 tsp oil, sprinkle mixed masala, and coriander leaves and cut into 12 pieces with a knife.

- Place each piece on top of the other covering the last piece from masala side down, press.

- Dust and roll again with a rolling pin to 6" diameter.

- Shallow-fry each *paratha* on a heated griddle (*tawa*) with 2 tbsp oil till light golden brown on both sides. Crush with palm. Serve hot.

- Masala *paratha* served with yoghurt and pickle makes a sumptuous mini meal.

- Masala *paratha* is also called 16-layered *paratha* because the dough is cut into 16 pieces before rolling for the second time.

PLAIN INDIAN BREAD
Sada Roti

INGREDIENTS

2 cups / 250 gm Wholewheat
flour (*atta*)
½ tsp / 2½ gm Salt
¾ cup / 150 ml Water to make
the dough
Clarified butter (*ghee*) for
applying

METHOD

- Sieve wholewheat flour with
  salt and knead to make a
  normal dough with water.
  Keep covered for 15 minutes.

- Divide the dough equally into
  12-15 balls, dust with wheat
  flour and roll with a rolling pin
  into 4" discs.

- Place on a heated griddle
  (*tawa*) and cook on both
  sides.

- Remove and roast over the
  flame directly till light golden
  brown.

- Apply ½ tsp clarified butter
  with a spoon and serve hot.

- Roasting can also be done on the griddle with the help of a napkin.
- Calorie watchers can omit applying clarified butter on the bread.

FENUGREEK BREAD
Besan Methi Roti

INGREDIENTS

1 cup / 100 gm Gram flour (*besan*)
½ cup / 65 gm Wholewheat flour (*atta*)
¼ tsp Baking soda
¾ tsp / 4 gm Salt
½ tsp / 2½ gm Red chilli powder
½ tsp / 2½ gm Carom (*ajwain*) seeds
a pinch Asafoetida (*hing*)
2 tbsp / 30 gm Yoghurt (*dahi*)
1 cup / 50 gm Fenugreek (*methi*) leaves, chopped
Clarified butter (*ghee*) for applying

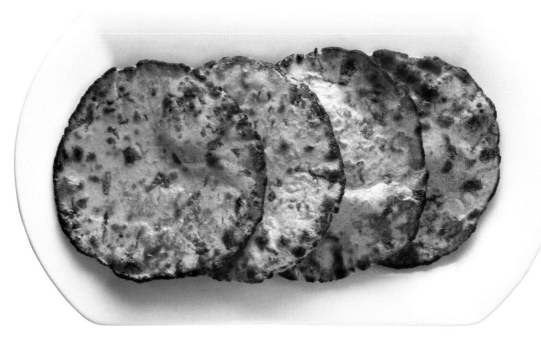

METHOD

- Sieve gram flour and wholewheat flour with baking soda and salt. Add red chilli powder, carom seeds, asafoetida, yoghurt, and fenugreek leaves; mix and prepare a semi-hard dough with water. Keep covered for 30 minutes.

- Divide the dough equally into 12 balls, dust each with wheat flour and roll with a rolling pin into 2½" disc.

- Place the disc on a heated griddle (*tawa*) and cook on both sides. Remove and roast over the flame directly till light brown.

- Apply ½ tsp clarified butter on each bread and serve hot.

- Gram flour consumes less water, hence it gets difficult to handle, if the dough is too soft.

- This bread made with wholewheat flour, gram flour, and fenugreek leaves has an unusual taste. It can be served for both lunch and dinner.

CRISP INDIAN BREAD
Khasta Roti

Serves: 2-4

INGREDIENTS

2 cups / 250 gm Wholewheat flour (*atta*)
1 tsp / 5 gm Salt
1 tbsp / 15 gm Clarified butter (*ghee*), melted
¾ cup / 150 ml Water to knead the dough
Carom (*ajwain*) seeds to sprinkle inside
Clarified butter for applying inside and outside

METHOD

• Sieve the wholewheat flour with salt. Add melted clarified butter and knead to make a semi-hard dough with water. Keep covered for 10 minutes.

• Divide the dough equally into 5 balls. Flatten each ball with a rolling pin, apply 1½ tsp clarified butter, sprinkle ¼ tsp carom seeds, and ¼ tsp wholewheat flour evenly.

• Fold from one end of the disc to another like a cylinder. Press the cylinder with the palm to form a string and fold the string like a flat ball (*peda*). Dust and roll with a rolling pin into a 6" disc. Repeat with the others.

• Place the disc on a heated griddle (*tawa*), turn after 30 seconds and prick with a fork evenly. Roast over medium flame until light golden brown. Remove, apply 1 tsp clarified butter on top and serve hot.

• *Khasta* roti goes well with any variety of lentil.
• This roti looks flat but it is actually very crisp to taste.

LENTIL PUFFS
Urad Dal Kachori

INGREDIENTS

2 cups / 250 gm Wholewheat flour (*atta*)
½ tsp / 2½ gm Salt
Water to make the dough
Vegetable oil for deep-frying

For the filling:
1 cup / 150 gm Black gram (*dhuli urad dal*), de-husked, split
¼ tsp Asafoetida (*hing*)
½ tsp / 2½ gm Salt
1 tsp / 5 gm Red chilli powder
2 tsp / 10 gm Fennel (*saunf*) powder
1 / 75 gm Potato, medium-sized, boiled, grated

METHOD

- Sieve the wholewheat flour with salt and knead to make a normal dough with water. Keep covered for 15 minutes.

- **For the filling**, wipe the black gram with napkin and grind to a fine powder. Mix with asafoetida, salt, red chilli powder, fennel powder, and ½ water. Keep covered for 30 minutes. Add potato, mix well and keep aside.

- Divide the dough and filling each into 20 portions. Flatten the portion of the dough slightly, place 1 tsp filling and fold to seal the filling inside.

- Dust with flour and roll with a rolling pin into 3½" discs.

- Heat 1"-deep oil in a pan; fry the discs in hot oil till they puff out and become light golden brown. Serve hot.

- *Urad dal kachori*, served with *aloo ka jhol* (see p. 108) and *meetha kaddu* (see p. 104), is usually prepared on festivals like Holi and Diwali.

- Black gram consumes a lot of water. After adding water to black gram paste, it may look watery initially, but will become thick after 30 minutes.

THICK FLOUR PUFFS
Bhatura

INGREDIENTS

2 cups / 250 gm All purpose flour (*maida*)
$^1/_3$ cup / 50 gm Semolina (*suji*)
¼ tsp Baking soda
½ tsp / 2½ gm Salt
½ tsp / 2½ gm Baking powder
2 tbsp / 30 gm Yoghurt (*dahi*), sour
1 tsp / 5 gm Sugar
Water to make the dough
Vegetable oil for deep-frying

METHOD

• Sieve the flour and semolina with baking soda, salt, and baking powder.

• Whisk yoghurt with sugar and add to the flour mixture. Mix and knead to make a soft dough with water. Keep covered for 3 hours with a moist napkin.

• Divide the dough equally into 15 portions, lightly dust with flour and roll into oblong shape to 5-6" diameter.

• Heat 1"-deep oil in a pan; fry the puff in hot oil till light golden brown. Serve hot.

• All purpose flour has an elastic texture and shrinks if not dusted with flour.
• *Bhatura* is served with *masala chana* (see p. 112), and is also accompanied with cut onions, pickle, and green chillies.
• Deep-fry the *bhatura* in hot oil otherwise they tend to consume more oil.

CAROM SPICED PUFFS
Namak Ajwain ki Puri

INGREDIENTS

2 cups / 250 gm Wholewheat flour (*atta*)
¾ tsp / 4 gm Salt
1 tsp / 5 gm Carom (*ajwain*) seeds
2 tsp / 10 gm Clarified butter (*ghee*), melted
Vegetable oil for deep-frying

METHOD

• Sieve wholewheat flour with salt. Add carom seeds and melted clarified butter; knead to make a hard dough with water. Keep covered for 15 minutes.

• Divide the dough equally into 18 balls. Roll each ball out with a rolling pin to 3½" diameter.

• Heat 1"-deep oil in a shallow pan; deep-fry the discs in hot oil until light golden brown. Serve hot.

• *Namak ajwain ki puri* tastes best with *jeera aloo* (see p. 87), and *aam ka kas* (see p. 165).

SPICY ROASTED INDIAN BREAD
Aloo Kulcha

INGREDIENTS

2 cups / 250 gm All purpose flour (*maida*)
½ tsp / 2½ gm Salt
¼ tsp Baking soda
½ tsp / 2½ gm Baking powder
2 tbsp / 30 gm Yoghurt (*dahi*)
2 tbsp / 30 ml Milk
½ tsp / 2½ gm Sugar
2 tbsp / 30 ml Vegetable oil
Water to make the dough
Butter for applying

For the filling: mix together
2 / 150 gm Potatoes, medium-sized, boiled, peeled, mashed
½ tsp / 2½ gm Red chilli powder
¼ tsp Mango powder (*amchur*)
¾ tsp / 4 gm Fennel (*saunf*) powder
¼ tsp Salt
2 tbsp Coriander (*dhaniya*) leaves, chopped

For the topping:
2 tbsp / 30 gm Onion seeds (*kalonji*)
2 tbsp Coriander leaves, chopped

METHOD

- Sieve the flour with salt, baking soda, and baking powder.

- Whisk the yoghurt with milk and sugar; add to the dough along with oil and knead to make an extra soft dough with water. Keep covered for 2 hours.

- Divide the dough equally into 12 balls, flatten slightly, fill with 1 tsp filling and fold to seal the filling inside.

- Sprinkle onion seeds and coriander leaves on a flat surface, press each ball over it. Dust and roll with a rolling pin into 4" disc.

- Heat the gas tandoor or pressure cooker and stick the *kulcha* with the help of water on the back side and cook till light golden brown. Remove, apply butter and serve hot. Alternately, you can bake in the oven at 200°C / 400°F for 4-6 minutes or until light brown.

- *Aloo kulcha* can be served with any kind of lentil or vegetable.
- A soft dough gives a good texture to the *kulcha*.
- Do not apply water on the onion seeds and coriander leaves side as this is the top side of the *kulcha*.

- *Kulcha* can be eaten with or without butter.
- This bread can also be made in a flat pan in emergencies like a normal stuffed roti.

ACCOMPANIMENTS

POTATOES IN YOGHURT
Aloo Raita

Serves: 4

INGREDIENTS

¾ cup Potatoes, boiled
(see p. 183), chopped
2 cups / 400 gm Yoghurt (*dahi*),
whisked
¼ cup / 50 ml Milk, chilled
Salt to taste
¼ tsp Ginger (*adrak*) paste
(see p. 191)
¼ tsp Green chilli paste
(see p. 191)
¼ tsp Coriander (*dhaniya*) paste
¼ tsp Black salt (*kala namak*)

For the garnishing:
½ tsp / 2½ gm Roasted cumin
(*jeera*) powder (see p. 184)
¼ tsp Red chilli powder
1 tbsp Coriander leaves,
chopped

METHOD

- Whisk the yoghurt and mix chilled milk, salt to taste, ginger paste, green chilli paste, coriander paste, and black salt.

- Add potatoes and mix.

- Serve chilled garnished with roasted cumin powder, red chilli powder, and coriander leaves.

- Always use chilled yoghurt.
- Adding ¼ cup chilled milk checks the sourness of yoghurt.

FRUITY YOGHURT
Anar aur Ananas Raita

INGREDIENTS

¼ cup Pomegranate seeds
(*anar dana*)

¾ cup Pineapple (*ananas*)
pieces, canned or fresh

2 cups / 400 gm Yoghurt (*dahi*),
whisked

¼ cup / 50 ml Milk, chilled

Salt to taste

¼ tsp Sugar, powdered

¼ tsp Mint (*pudina*) powder
(see p. 11) Or

½ tsp / 2½ gm Mint paste

¼ tsp Black pepper (*kali mirch*)

For the garnishing:

¼ tsp Roasted cumin (*jeera*)
powder (see p. 184)

1 tbsp Coriander (*dhaniya*)
leaves, chopped

METHOD

- Whisk the yoghurt and mix
  chilled milk, salt to taste, sugar,
  mint powder or paste, and
  black pepper.

- Add pineapple and
  pomegranate seeds; mix.

- Serve chilled garnished with
  roasted cumin powder and
  coriander leaves.

- Any yoghurt preparation, without cooking, mixed with herbs, fruits or
  vegetables, seasoned with salt, and served chilled is called *raita*.

- *Raita* has a cooling effect, hence is a good accompaniment to balance
  a spicy dish.

YOGHURT WITH LENTIL PEARLS
Boondi Raita

INGREDIENTS

¾ cup Gram flour pearls
(*boondi*)
2 cups / 400 gm Yoghurt (*dahi*),
whisked
¼ cup / 50 ml Milk, chilled
Salt to taste

For the garnishing:

½ tsp / 2½ gm Roasted cumin
(*jeera*) powder (see p. 184)
¼ tsp Red chilli powder
1 tbsp Coriander (*dhaniya*)
leaves, chopped

METHOD

• Whisk yoghurt with chilled milk, salt to taste, and gram flour pearls.

• Serve chilled garnished with roasted cumin powder, red chilli powder, and coriander leaves.

• This *raita* is commonly accompanied with any kind of stuffed *paratha*.
• *Boondi* can be soaked in 2½ cups water for half an hour; squeezed and then used. This helps to remove excess oil.
• *Boondi* packets are readily available in grocery stores.
• To prepare *boondi* at home see p. 168.

LENTIL DUMPLINGS IN CREAMY YOGHURT
Dahi Pakodi

Serves: 4

INGREDIENTS

¾ cup / 125 gm Green gram (*moong dal*), washed, soaked in plenty of water for 3 hours, drained

1½ tbsp / 25 gm Black gram (*urad dal*), washed, soaked in plenty of water for 3 hours, drained

5 cups / 1 lt Yoghurt (*dahi*), hung (see p. 198)

½-1 cup / 100-200 ml Milk, chilled

Salt to taste

Vegetable oil for deep-frying

Red chilli powder to taste

Roasted cumin (*jeera*) powder (see p. 184) to taste

Coriander (*dhaniya*) leaves, chopped for garnishing

METHOD

- Place the yoghurt in a strainer for 2 hours, discard the water, remove from strainer and whisk. Add chilled milk to get a medium-thick consistency. Add salt to taste and refrigerate.

- Grind the lentils together with minimum water to get a thick consistency. Beat the mixture till light and fluffy.

- Heat 1"-deep oil in a shallow pan; drop small portions of batter with your fingers, a few at a time, and deep-fry in hot oil to light golden brown.

- Immerse the balls in 5 cups salted water for an hour. Squeeze within the palm to remove excess water, keep aside and refrigerate.

- Place squeezed balls in a serving dish and cover with yoghurt mixture. Sprinkle red chilli powder, cumin powder, and coriander leaves and serve chilled. It is served along with sweet chutney (see p. 157) and green chutney (see p.154).

- Slightly coarse ground lentil gives a better texture to *dahi pakodi*.
- For salted water, mix 1 tsp salt in 5 cups water.

- *Dahi pakodi* is an integral part of a formal family meal in north India which is served chilled.

YOGHURT WITH GRATED BOTTLE GOURD
Lauki Raita

INGREDIENTS

200 gm Bottle gourd (*lauki*),
peeled, grated
2 cups / 400 gm Yoghurt (*dahi*)
¼ cup / 50 ml Milk, chilled
Salt to taste

For the garnishing:
½ tsp / 2½ gm Roasted cumin
(*jeera*) powder (see p. 184)
¼ tsp Red chilli powder
1 tbsp Coriander (*dhaniya*)
leaves, chopped

METHOD

• Pressure cook grated bottle
  gourd with 2 cups water to
  one whistle. Cool, drain and
  squeeze.

• Whisk yoghurt, add chilled
  milk, salt to taste, and
  squeezed bottle gourd; mix.

• Serve chilled garnished with
  roasted cumin powder, red
  chilli powder, and coriander
  leaves.

• For variation, grated and cooked red pumpkin can be used instead of
  bottle gourd.

LIQUID YOGHURT SALAD
Kachumar Raita

INGREDIENTS

½ cup / 75 gm Cucumber
(*khira*), chopped
¼ cup / 50 gm Onion, chopped
¼ cup / 50 gm Tomatoes,
chopped
2 cups / 400 gm Yoghurt (*dahi*)
¼ cup / 50 ml Milk, chilled
½ tsp / 2½ gm Green chilli
paste (see p. 191)
Salt to taste

For the garnishing:

½ tsp / 2½ gm Roasted cumin
(*jeera*) powder (see p. 184)
1 tbsp Coriander (*dhaniya*)
leaves, chopped

METHOD

- Whisk yoghurt, add chilled
  milk, green chilli paste, and salt
  to taste; mix.

- Add cucumber, onion, and
  tomatoes; mix.

- Serve chilled garnished with
  roasted cumin powder and
  coriander leaves.

- This *raita* can be served with any meal but it is a must with *dal biryani*
  (see p. 128).

TEMPERED LIQUID YOGHURT
Tarka Mattha

Serves: 4-6

INGREDIENTS

2½ cups / 500 gm Yoghurt
(*dahi*)
¾ cup / 150 ml Water
Salt to taste
¼ tsp Ginger (*adrak*) paste
(see p. 191)
¼ tsp Green chilli paste
(see p. 191)
1 tsp / 5 gm Coriander
(*dhaniya*) paste
For the tempering:
2 tsp / 10 ml Vegetable oil
a pinch Asafoetida (*hing*)
¼ tsp Mustard seeds (*rai*)
2 Dry red chillies (*sookhi lal mirch*)
6 Curry leaves (*kadhi patta*)

METHOD

- Whisk yoghurt and add ¾ cup water.

- Add salt to taste, ginger paste, green chilli paste, and coriander paste; mix well.

- **For the tempering**, heat 2 tsp oil in a pan for 30 seconds; add asafoetida, mustard seeds, dry red chillies, and curry leaves.

- Pour over the yoghurt mixture and serve chilled.

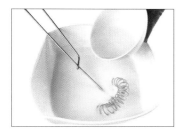
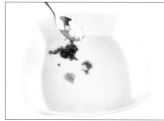

- Slightly sour yoghurt is preferred for better taste.

- Such accompaniments make a meal interesting.

SPINACH FLAVOURED YOGHURT
Palak Raita

INGREDIENTS

1½ cups / 75 gm Spinach (*palak*), chopped
2 cups / 400 gm Yoghurt (*dahi*)
¼ cup / 50 ml Milk, chilled
Salt to taste

For the tempering:

¼ tsp Clarified butter (*ghee*)
a pinch Asafoetida (*hing*)
½ tsp / 2½ gm Cumin (*jeera*) seeds
2 Dry red chillies (*sookhi lal mirch*)

METHOD

* Heat the pan for 30 seconds; add chopped spinach and cook covered for a minute (see p. 196). Remove and cool. Pound spinach to make a paste.

* Whisk yoghurt and add milk, salt to taste, and spinach paste; mix.

* **For the tempering,** heat ¼ tsp clarified butter in a pan; add asafoetida, cumin seeds, and dry red chillies. Pour over the yoghurt and serve chilled.

* For variation, use 2 tsp mint paste instead of spinach to make mint *raita*. Mint needs no cooking.

GREEN CHUTNEY
Hari Chutney

INGREDIENTS

2 cups / 100 gm Coriander
(*dhaniya*) leaves, washed,
drained in a colander
2 tsp / 10 gm Green chillies,
chopped
½ tsp / 2½ gm Cumin (*jeera*)
seeds
a pinch Asafoetida (*hing*)
½ tsp / 2½ gm Coriander
(*dhaniya*) powder
1 tsp / 5 gm Salt
Lemon (*nimbu*) juice to taste

METHOD

* Grind coriander leaves,
  green chillies, cumin seeds,
  asafoetida, coriander powder,
  and salt with minimum water
  to make a smooth paste.

* Transfer into a bowl.

* Add lemon juice just before
  serving.

* Lemon juice added to the chutney, just before serving, gives a fresh
  green colour, but it fades after sometime because of the alkaline
  reaction of lemon.

CHERRY TOMATO CHUTNEY
Chhote Tamatar ki Chutney

INGREDIENTS

300 gm Cherry tomatoes, make
a cross on each
2 tsp / 10 ml Vegetable oil
a pinch Asafoetida (*hing*)
2 tsp / 10 gm Ginger (*adrak*),
chopped
1 Green chilli, slit
1 tbsp Raisins (*kishmish*)
Salt to taste
1½ tsp / 8 gm Sugar
¼ tsp Black pepper (*kali mirch*)
½ tsp / 2½ gm Roasted cumin
(*jeera*) powder (see p. 184)
1 tbsp Mint (*pudina*), chopped

METHOD

- Boil 3½ cups water; add tomatoes and cook for 2 minutes, uncovered. Drain in a colander. Cool and peel.

- Heat 2 tsp oil in a pan for 30 seconds; add asafoetida, ginger, green chilli, and raisins.

- Add peeled tomatoes, ¼ cup water, salt to taste, and sugar; bring to the boil, and simmer for 5 minutes.

- Add black pepper, roasted cumin powder, and mint; mix well. Serve hot.

- Making a cross on the tomatoes makes it easier to peel.
- It can also be prepared with large tomatoes. In such case, cut the tomatoes into 1" cubes after peeling.

COCONUT CHUTNEY
Nariyal ki Chutney

INGREDIENTS

1 cup / 50 gm Coconut (*nariyal*), fresh, grated

½ cup / 50 gm Bengal gram (*chana dal*), de-husked, split, roasted

2 tsp / 10 gm Green chillies, chopped

½ tsp / 2½ gm Salt

¾-1 cup / 150-200 ml Water to blend

2 tbsp Coriander (*dhaniya*) leaves, chopped

For the tempering:

1 tbsp / 15 ml Vegetable oil

½ tsp / 2½ gm Bengal gram, de-husked, split

½ tsp / 2½ gm Split black gram (*dhuli urad dal*), de-husked

¼ tsp Mustard seeds (*rai*)

2 Dry red chillies (*sookhi lal mirch*)

8 Curry leaves (*kadhi patta*)

METHOD

• Blend coconut, roasted Bengal gram, green chillies, salt, and water to a smooth paste in a food processor. Add coriander leaves and blend again for 10 seconds.

• Transfer to a bowl and keep aside.

• **For the tempering**, heat 1 tbsp oil in a pan for 30 seconds; add the lentils and cook till light brown. Add mustard seeds, dry red chillies, and curry leaves. Remove and pour over the chutney and serve.

• This chutney is generally served with south Indian snacks such as *idli, upma,* etc.

• Coconut chutney is always prepared fresh for authentic flavour.

• Leftover chutney should be refrigerated.

• Roasted Bengal gram is available in grocery stores.

SWEET CHUTNEY
Meethi Chutney

Makes: 1½ cups

INGREDIENTS

1½ cups / 300 gm Jaggery (*gur*), broken into small pieces
2 tbsp / 30 gm Mango powder (*amchur*)
1½ tsp / 8 gm Salt

For masala A:

1 tsp / 5 gm *Garam* masala (see p. 184)
2 tsp / 10 gm Roasted cumin (*jeera*) powder (see p. 184)
1 tsp / 5 gm Black salt (*kala namak*)

For masala B:

¹/₈ tsp Asafoetida (*hing*)
2 tsp / 10 gm Coriander (*dhaniya*) powder
2 tsp / 10 gm Red chilli powder

METHOD

- Mix jaggery with 1½ cups water in a pan and cook, on low heat, till it dissolves. Strain and keep aside.

- Mix mango powder in 1½ cups water.

- Mix jaggery water with mango water. Add salt and bring to the boil, simmer for 40 minutes. Remove and cool.

- Dry roast masala B ingredients in a pan, till light golden brown. Keep aside.

- Add masala A and masala B to the cooked jaggery and mango powder mixture and mix well.

- *Meethi* chutney can be stored in the refrigerator for up to a month.
- It can be served with any snack.

JAGGERY FLAVOURED MANGO CHUTNEY
Aam ki Launji

INGREDIENTS

500 gm Raw mangoes (*kairi*), peeled, cut into 1" cubes
2 tbsp / 30 gm Jaggery (*gur*), powdered
1 tbsp / 15 ml Vegetable oil
$\frac{1}{8}$ tsp Asafoetida (*hing*)
¼ tsp Fenugreek seeds (*methi dana*)
¼ tsp Cumin (*jeera*) seeds
¼ tsp Fennel (*saunf*) seeds
1 tsp / 5 gm Red chilli powder
1 tsp / 5 gm Turmeric (*haldi*) powder
1 tsp / 5 gm Fennel powder
½ tsp / 2½ gm Salt
¼ cup / 50 ml Water

METHOD

• Heat 1 tbsp oil in a pan for 30 seconds on medium heat; add asafoetida, fenugreek seeds, cumin seeds, and fennel seeds. Add red chilli powder, turmeric powder, fennel powder, and cut mangoes; mix well.

• Add salt and ¼ cup water; cook, covered, on low heat, till mangoes are slightly soft. Add jaggery and cook, covered, for 2 minutes on low heat. Remove and serve.

• *Aam ki launji* has a tangy flavour.
• This *chutney* can last in the fridge for up to 15 days.

• All kinds of *paratha* can be enjoyed with this chutney.

FRESH MANGO PICKLE
Aam ka Tazaa Achaar

Serves: 8-10

INGREDIENTS

2 / 250 gm Raw mangoes (*kairi*), cut into medium-sized cubes with skin
2 tsp / 10 gm Mustard seeds (*rai*)
½ tsp / 2½ gm Fenugreek seeds (*methi dana*)
4 tsp / 20 gm Fennel (*saunf*) powder
2 tsp / 10 gm Coriander (*dhaniya*) powder
¾ tsp / 4 gm Turmeric (*haldi*) powder
2 tsp / 10 gm Red chilli powder
3 tsp / 15 gm Salt
1 tbsp / 15 ml White vinegar (*sirka*)
2 tbsp / 30 ml Mustard (*sarson*) oil

METHOD

- Grind mustard seeds and fenugreek seeds together.
- Mix the ground seeds with fennel powder, coriander powder, turmeric powder, red chilli powder, salt, white vinegar, and mustard oil to form a masala paste.
- Mix the masala paste with mango pieces and leave aside for 2 hours. Serve.

- Refrigerate for later use. But consume within 30 days.

- Mixed masala paste can be stored for up to 6 months in the refrigerator.

LEMON FLAVOURED GINGER
Nimbu ka Adrak

INGREDIENTS

¾ cup / 150 gm Ginger (*adrak*),
peeled, cut into 1"-long pieces
2 tsp / 10 gm Salt
2 tbsp / 30 ml Lemon (*nimbu*)
juice

METHOD

- Mix the cut ginger with
  salt and lemon juice; leave
  aside for 30 minutes at
  room temperature, covered.
  Refrigerate and serve.

- Ginger turns pink in colour after left mixed with lemon juice and salt.
- Refrigerate for later use.

TANGY RADISH FLAKES
Mooli ka Kas

Serves: 4-6

INGREDIENTS

1 cup / 200 gm Radish (*mooli*), peeled, grated
2 tsp / 10 gm Salt
1½ tbsp / 25 gm Ginger (*adrak*), peeled, grated
2 tsp / 10 gm Green chillies, chopped
1 tbsp Coriander (*dhaniya*) leaves, chopped
1 tbsp / 15 ml Lemon (*nimbu*) juice

METHOD

- Mix the grated radish with 1½ tsp salt; leave aside for 2 minutes, squeeze and discard the water.

- Mix squeezed radish with ginger, green chillies, coriander leaves, ½ tsp salt, and lemon juice. Refrigerate and serve.

- Radish is high in water content. Adding salt and squeezing later improves the texture and prevents the radish from getting watery.

- Normally *mooli ka kas* is served during lunch time.

GREEN CHILLI PICKLE
Hari Mirch ka Achaar

INGREDIENTS

125 gm Green chillies, thick, large, washed, wiped dry, slit vertically, keeping shape intact, deseeded
¾ tbsp / 11 gm Salt
½ tbsp / 8 gm Fenugreek seeds (*methi dana*)
1 tbsp / 15 gm Mustard seeds (*rai*)
2 tbsp / 30 gm Fennel (*saunf*) powder
1½ tsp / 8 gm Turmeric (*haldi*) powder
2 tsp / 10 gm Coriander (*dhaniya*) powder
1½ tbsp / 25 ml Lemon (*nimbu*) juice
¼ tsp Asafoetida (*hing*)
2 tbsp / 30 ml Mustard (*sarson*) oil
2 tsp / 10 ml White vinegar (*sirka*)

METHOD

- Grind fenugreek seeds and mustard seeds together to a fine powder in a food processor; remove. Mix this powder with fennel powder, turmeric powder, coriander powder, lemon juice, asafoetida, 1 tbsp mustard oil, and white vinegar.

- Stuff each chilli evenly with this mixed masala.

- Apply 1 tbsp oil on the stuffed chillies and consume after 2 days.

- *Hari mirch ka achaar* should be consumed within 7 days. For extended use, refrigerate to avoid deterioration.

QUICK GREEN CHILLI PICKLE
Jhatpat Hari Mirch ka Achaar

INGREDIENTS

100 gm Green chillies, washed, wiped-dry, slit vertically

For the filling: mix and keep aside

4 tsp / 20 gm *Chaat* masala

1 tsp / 5 gm Salt

For the seasoning:

1½ tbsp / 25 ml Mustard (*sarson*) oil

a pinch Asafoetida (*hing*)

¼ tsp Fenugreek seeds (*methi dana*)

¼ tsp Cumin (*jeera*) seeds

2 tsp / 10 gm Gram flour (*besan*)

Other Ingredients

1 tsp / 5 gm Coriander (*dhaniya*) powder

2 tsp / 10 gm Fennel (*saunf*) powder

½ tsp / 2½ gm Mango powder (*amchur*)

¼ tsp Salt

METHOD

- Fill each green chilli evenly with the filling mixture.

- Heat 1½ tbsp oil in a pan for 30 seconds on medium heat; add asafoetida, fenugreek seeds, cumin seeds, and gram flour; cook for 10 seconds.

- Add stuffed green chillies and mix.

- Add coriander powder, fennel powder, mango powder, and salt; cook on high heat for a minute, stirring constantly. Remove and serve.

- This chilli is spicy with a pungent flavour.
- Adding gram flour to this pickle brings out its true flavour

PICKLED ONIONS
Sirkewale Pyaz

INGREDIENTS

2 / 150 gm Onions, medium-sized, cut into 1" cubes, layers separated

2 tbsp / 30 ml White / Balsamic vinegar (*sirka*)

1½ tsp / 8 gm Salt

½ cup / 100 ml Water

METHOD

• Mix the onions with white / balsamic vinegar, salt, and water; leave aside, covered, for an hour. Serve.

• Pearl onions can also be used instead of regular onions.
• Discard water before serving.

• It can be served with any meal.
• Onions turn dark pink when mixed with vinegar.

MANGO MARMALADE
Aam ka Kas

Makes: 2 cups

INGREDIENTS

1 kg Raw mangoes (*kairi*)
3 cups / 600 gm Sugar
2 tbsp / 30 gm Salt
¼ tsp Asafoetida (*hing*)
1 tsp / 5 gm *Garam* masala
(see p. 184)

METHOD

• Peel and grate the mangoes.

• Mix the grated mangoes with sugar and salt. Keep covered for 30 minutes.

• Cook on medium heat, stirring occasionally, to one string consistency (see p. 200).

• Turn off the heat, add asafoetida and *garam* masala; mix well. Cool and store in an airtight jar.

• *Aam ka kas* can be stored for up to six months
• This marmalade is served with meals.

• It has a unique sweet and sour flavour.

DESSERTS

SUNRISE PUDDING
Boondi Bake

INGREDIENTS

6 Bread slices
1 cup / 200 gm Gram flour (*besan*)
Clarified butter (*ghee*) for deep-frying
¾ cup / 150 gm Sugar
½ tsp / 2½ gm Green cardamom (*choti elaichi*), powdered
¼ tsp Saffron (*kesar*)
1½ cups / 300 ml Milk
1¼ cups / 250 ml Cream (see p. 200)
2 tbsp Almonds (*badam*), blanched, chopped (see p. 202)
2 tbsp Pistachios (*pista*), blanched, chopped (see p. 202)

METHOD

- Remove the sides of the bread with a sharp knife, toast them lightly in a toaster, without browning. Keep aside.

- Combine gram flour with ¾ cup water and prepare a semi-thick batter. Heat 1½"-deep clarified butter in a shallow pan; pour the batter through a *boondi* spatula and fry till light golden brown. Remove and keep aside.

- Mix the sugar with ¼ cup water in a pan and cook on medium heat, stirring occasionally, to one-string consistency (see p. 200); turn off the heat. Add green cardamom and saffron powder (see p. 203); mix well.

- Add the fried *boondi* to the sugar syrup, mix till well coated; cool. Grind coarsely in a food processor. Keep aside.

- Arrange the bread slices in an 8" square dish, cover with *boondi* and pour milk evenly over it. Bake in the oven at 140°C / 275°F for 10-15 minutes or until light brown.

- Remove decorate with double whipped cream, almonds, and pistachios. Serve immediately.

- This popular Indian dessert is a melody of crunchy baked *boondi* and chilled cream.

- Indian desserts should always be prepared in clarified butter for better taste.

FRUIT AND CUSTARD PUDDING
Thanda Phalon ka Custard

INGREDIENTS

1 packet Orange jelly
2 tsp / 10 gm Butter
6 Marie biscuit crumbs
(see p. 199)
4 tbsp Custard powder
5 cups / 1 lt Milk
4 tbsp / 60 gm Sugar
4 cups Mixed fruits, chopped
(orange, banana, apples)

METHOD

- Set the jelly as per packet instructions and refrigerate (see p. 201).

- Melt 2 tsp butter in a pan, mix with biscuit crumbs. Remove and press in a 6" shallow serving dish. Leave in the refrigerator for 45 minutes to set.

- Mix the custard powder in ½ cup milk. Keep aside.

- Mix the remaining 4½ cups milk with sugar in a pan and bring to the boil on medium heat. Add custard powder mixture and stir constantly to one boil. Turn off the heat, cool and chill.

- To arrange, remove the chilled biscuit crumb dish from the fridge, spoon the chilled custard over the crumbs, cover with chopped fruits and top with set jelly. Serve chilled.

- Fruit and custard pudding is very popular among teenage kids.
- Custard powder should be mixed in room temperature milk, or else it gets lumpy.
- Hot custard can also be served in winter with cakes.
- Set jelly can be cut with a sharp knife to any size desired.

INDIAN RICE PUDDING
Chawal ki Kheer

INGREDIENTS

2 tbsp / 30 gm Basmati rice
¼ tsp Saffron (*kesar*)
4 Green cardamom (*choti elaichi*), deseeded
¼ tsp Clarified butter (*ghee*)
7½ cups / 1½ lt Milk
4 tbsp / 60 gm Sugar
2 tbsp Almonds (*badam*), blanched, chopped (see p. 202)
2 tbsp Pistachios (*pista*), blanched, chopped (see p. 202)

METHOD

- Wash and soak the rice in plenty of water for 10 minutes; drain. Keep aside.

- Pound saffron and green cardamom together to a fine powder (see p. 203).

- Heat ¼ tsp clarified butter in a heavy-bottom vessel; add soaked rice and cook for a minute. Add milk and bring to the boil. Reduce heat and cook till the mixture is reduced to $\frac{1}{3}$rd its original consistency, stirring occasionally.

- Add sugar and cook for 10 minutes on low heat. Add cardamom and saffron powder and turn off the heat. Cool and refrigerate the mixture. Serve chilled garnished with almonds and pistachios.

- This is a popular easy-to-make Indian dessert.
- *Kheer* can be served either hot or cold.

- *Kheer* can be made one day in advance and kept in the fridge.
- Blanched and chopped almonds and pistachios add to the flavour.

VERMICELLI PUDDING
Sewai ki Kheer

Serves: 4-6

INGREDIENTS

½ cup / 50 gm Vermicelli (*sewai*)
6 cups / 1¼ lt Milk
3 Green cardamom (*choti elaichi*), deseeded
¼ tsp Saffron (*kesar*)
½ tsp / 2½ gm Clarified butter (*ghee*)
2-3 tbsp / 30-45 gm Sugar
2 tbsp Raisins (*kishmish*)
2 tbsp Pistachios (*pista*), blanched, chopped (see p. 202)

METHOD

• Pound green cardamom and saffron to a powder (see p. 203). Keep aside.

• Heat ½ tsp clarified butter in a shallow pan for 30 seconds; add vermicelli and cook on low heat, stirring constantly, till light golden brown. Add milk and bring to the boil. Reduce heat and simmer for 30 minutes.

• Add sugar and raisins; cook for 5 minutes, turn off the heat.

• Add cardamom and saffron powder; mix. Serve hot or cold garnished with pistachios.

• This is a quick dessert to make on a short notice.

• Vermicelli packets are easily available in Indian grocery stores.

SWEET SAFFRON RICE
Meetha Kesari Chawal

Serves: 4-6

INGREDIENTS
125 gm Basmati rice
½ tsp / 2½ gm Green cardamom (*choti elaichi*), deseeded
¼ tsp Saffron (*kesar*)
125 gm Sugar
¼ cup / 50 ml Water
½ cup Almonds (*badam*) blanched (see p. 202), cut lengthwise
2 tbsp Pistachios (*pista*) blanched (see p. 202), cut lengthwise
¼ cup / 50 gm Clarified butter (*ghee*)
2 Cloves (*laung*)

METHOD
- Wash and soak the rice in plenty of water for 30 minutes, drain. Cook in boiling water till done and strain (see p. 190).

- Pound green cardamom and saffron to a fine powder (see p. 203). Keep aside.

- Mix sugar and water in a pan and cook on low heat to two-string consistency (see p. 200). Turn off the heat, add ¾th amount of both cut almonds and pistachios. Add powdered saffron and cardamom and cooked rice to the syrup; mix and leave covered for 2 hours. Stir occasionally.

- Heat ¼ cup clarified butter in a pan for 30 seconds; add cloves and when it begins to change colour remove and add this seasoning to the rice mixture. Mix gently.

- Serve hot or cold, garnished with remaining almonds and pistachios.

- Boiled rice added to sugar syrup leaves water initially, but soaks up after 2 hours.

- *Meetha kesari chawal* is a delicacy and is generally served along with meals.

CARROT PUDDING
Gajar ka Halwa

INGREDIENTS

1 kg Carrots (*gajar*), peeled, grated
5 cups / 1 lt Milk
1¼ cups / 250 gm Sugar
125 gm Wholemilk fudge (*khoya*)
4 tbsp / 60 gm Clarified butter (*ghee*)
1 tsp / 5 gm Green cardamom (*choti elaichi*) powder
½ cup Cashew nuts (*kaju*), chopped
½ cup Almonds (*badam*), blanched, chopped (see p. 202)
¼ cup Pistachios (*pista*), blanched, chopped (see p. 202)

METHOD

- Combine the grated carrot with milk in a large pan and cook on medium heat, stirring occasionally, till the milk evaporates.

- Add sugar and cook on low heat till the mixture is semi-thick, turning frequently.

- Add grated wholemilk fudge and cook on low heat for 10 minutes, turning frequently.

- Add clarified butter and cook on low heat, turning constantly for 15 minutes. Turn off the heat, add cardamom powder and chopped cashew nuts; mix well.

- Serve hot, garnished with almonds and pistachios.

- Discard the hard centre portion of the carrots while grating.
- Carrot pudding can be stored in the fridge for up to a week.

- Red carrots can also be used instead of the orange ones. In fact, red carrots consume less sugar as they are sweeter in taste.

HOT SEMOLINA PUDDING
Suji Halwa

INGREDIENTS

¾ cup / 125 gm Semolina (*suji*)
6 Green cardamom (*choti elaichi*), deseeded
¼ tsp Saffron (*kesar*) strands
¾ cup / 150 gm Sugar
375 ml Water
5 tbsp / 75 gm Clarified butter (*ghee*)
2 tbsp / 30 gm Gram flour (*besan*)
¼ cup Almonds (*badam*), blanched, chopped (see p. 202)
2 tbsp Pistachios (*pista*), blanched, chopped (see p. 202)

METHOD

• Pound green cardamom and saffron into a fine powder (see p. 203). Keep aside.

• Prepare sugar syrup by mixing sugar and water in a pan and boiling the mixture, on low heat, till the sugar dissolves. Keep aside.

• Heat 4 tbsp clarified butter in a shallow pan for a minute; add semolina and gram flour and fry on low heat, till light golden brown, stirring frequently.

• Add sugar syrup and stir constantly, on low heat, till the mixture becomes semi-thick.

• Add cardamom and saffron powder, mix. Add the remaining 1 tbsp clarified butter and mix. Serve hot garnished with almonds and pistachios.

• Water should be added to fried semolina 30 minutes before serving, otherwise the pudding becomes too thick.

• Adding 1 tbsp clarified butter later improves the texture of the pudding.

SAFFRON PISTACHIO DELIGHT
Kesar Pista Kulfi

Serves: 6-8

INGREDIENTS

10 cups / 2 lt Milk
5 tbsp / 75 gm Sugar
¼ tsp Saffron (*kesar*)
8 Green cardamom (*choti elaichi*), deseeded
2 tbsp Pistachios (*pista*), blanched, chopped (see p. 202)
8 *Kulfi* moulds

METHOD

• Pound saffron and green cardamom to a fine powder (see p. 203).

• Heat the milk in a shallow pan and cook on medium heat till reduced to ¼ th its original consistency, stirring occasionally.

• Add sugar and cook for 2 minutes. Turn off the heat. Add saffron-cardamom powder to the condensed hot milk; mix well and cool.

• Mix the milk mixture with 1½ tbsp pistachios and blend in a mixer for 10 seconds. Pour into the *kulfi* moulds, sprinkle remaining pistachios on top, cover the moulds with the lid and deep freeze for 10-12 hours or until set.

• De-mould set *kulfi* with a sharp knife. Remove to a plate, cut into slices and serve.

• Use full-cream milk for better taste.
• It can also be made with skimmed milk for weight watchers.

• For easy unmoulding, wash the frozen *kulfi* moulds under running water.

SWEET COCONUT SQUARES
Nariyal Burfi

INGREDIENTS

450 gm Coconut (*nariyal*), fresh, grated
2¼ cups / 450 gm Sugar
200 gm Wholemilk fudge (*khoya*), grated
1 tbsp / 15 ml Rose water (*gulab jal*)
Silver leaves (*varq*) for decoration
2 tbsp Almonds (*badam*), blanched, chopped (see p. 202)
2 tbsp Pistachios (*pista*), blanched, chopped (see p. 202)

METHOD

- Mix grated coconut with sugar and leave for 30 minutes in a shallow pan. Cook on medium heat, mixing constantly, till a sugar coating is seen on the surface, while turning.

- Add grated wholemilk fudge and rose water; mix well.

- Transfer to a greased tray (8" x 4") and press down immediately. Leave to set for 4 hours.

- Decorate with silver leaves, almonds and pistachios and cut into square pieces. Serve.

- Select medium-ripe coconuts and scrape south-Indian style.
- Silver leaves are mainly used for decoration, and do not contribute to the taste.

- For the sugar coating to form it takes 20-30 minutes.
- This Indian sweet can be kept for up to a week. It is an ideal preparation for Holi, Diwali, and other festivals.

SWEET DIAMONDS
Shakkar Pare

INGREDIENTS

2 cups / 250 gm All purpose flour (*maida*)

3 tbsp / 45 gm Clarified butter (*ghee*) melted

Lukewarm water to make the dough

2½ cups / 500 gm Clarified butter for deep-frying

1 cup / 200 gm Sugar

⅓ cup / 65 ml Water

METHOD

- Sieve the flour; add 3 tbsp melted ghee and knead to prepare a hard dough with lukewarm water. Keep aside covered for 10 minutes.

- Divide the dough into 2 equal balls, roll each ball into ¼"-thick disc and cut into ½" cubes.

- Heat 2½ cups clarified butter in a shallow, frying pan till medium-hot; add the cubes and deep-fry till light golden brown. Remove and cool.

- Prepare sugar syrup with sugar and water to one-string consistency (see p. 200); turn off the heat.

- Add fried cubes into the sugar syrup and keep mixing until sugar coating is formed on the cubes. Remove, cool and store.

- This Indian sweet is particularly made on the festival of colours, Holi.
- It can be stored for up to 20 days in a cool, dry place.

SWEET DUMPLINGS LACED IN SYRUP
Gulab Jamun

INGREDIENTS

250 gm Wholemilk fudge
(*khoya*)
60 gm Cottage cheese (*paneer*)
¼ cup / 30 gm All purpose flour
(*maida*)
2¼ cups / 450 gm Sugar
2¼ cups / 450 ml Water
2½ cups / 500 gm Clarified
butter (*ghee*) for deep-frying

METHOD

• Prepare sugar syrup by mixing sugar and water in a pan and boiling the mixture, on low heat, cook till the sugar dissolves, strain Keep aside.

• Mash wholemilk fudge and cottage cheese to a smooth paste separately, with a rolling stone. Mix the two pastes with flour and prepare a soft dough.

• Divide the dough equally into 20-25 portions and shape them into round balls.

• Heat 2½ cups clarified butter in a shallow pan on low heat; add 15 balls at a time, and watch till they float, increase heat to high and cook till golden brown, turning frequently and gently with the spatula.

• Remove, add them to the sugar syrup and leave for an hour. Reheat with sugar syrup and serve hot.

• *Khoya* also called *khawa* or *mawa* is a common ingredient in many traditional Indian sweets. When milk is slowly evaporated under heat, it eventually becomes a solid mass which is called *khoya*.

• *Gulab Jamun* is a popular Indian dessert
• *Gulab jamun* can last for up to 10-15 days in the fridge.
• It can also be stuffed with chopped almonds and pistachios.

COOKING PROCESSES

BAKING POTATOES AND SWEET POTATOES

• Apply oil on the sweet potatoes.

• Apply oil on the potatoes.

• Bake at 200°C / 400°F for 20-30 minutes or until soft.

• Bake at 200°C / 400°F for 20-30 minutes or until soft.

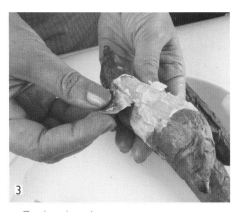

• Cool and peel.

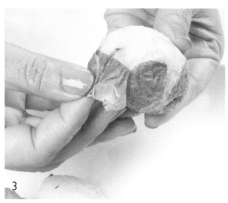

• Cool and peel.

BAKING TIP

• Applying oil on the potatoes / sweet potatoes, helps to remove the skin easily.

PRESSURE COOKING POTATOES / RAW BANANAS / RAW MANGOES

- Place raw potatoes in the pressure cooker, add enough water to cover, cook to one whistle. Simmer for 4 minutes.

- Place raw bananas in the pressure cooker, add enough water to cover, cook to one whistle.

- Place raw mangoes in the pressure cooker, add enough water to cover, cook to one whistle.

- Cool and drain.

- Simmer for 4 minutes. Cool and drain.

- Simmer for 4 minutes. Cool and drain.

- Peel and use as per recipe

- Peel or mash and use as per recipe

PREPARING SPICE MIXES

Chana Masala

- Mix together 2 tbsp coriander seeds, 2 tsp cumin seeds, 5 cloves, 1" cinnamon stick, 2 deseeded black cardamom, 8 black peppercorns, and 4 dry red chillies.

SPICE TIP
- These spice mixes can be stored for up to two weeks.

- Dry roast all the spices on low heat, till light golden brown.
- Cool and grind coarsely.

Roasted Cumin Powder

- Roast 2 tbsp cumin seeds in a pan, on low heat, stirring frequently, till golden brown.

Garam Masala

- Mix together 2 tbsp black peppercorns, 8 deseeded black cardamom, and 2 tsp cloves.

- Store in an airtight jar.

- Cool and grind coarsely.

- Grind to a powder.

Peanut Powder

- Heat 2 tbsp oil in a pan till medium-hot; add ½ cup peanuts and fry till light brown. Remove and cool.

Roasting Semolina

- Dry roast semolina in a shallow pan for 5 minutes on low heat; remove.

Roasting Vermicelli

Magori

Magoris are sun-dried split green gram dumplings. They are made by soaking and grinding split green gram, shaping them into small balls and drying in the sun.

- Deep-fry *magoris* in medium-hot oil till light golden brown.

2

- Remove the skin with fingers.

- Heat the clarified butter (as per recipe) in a pan for 30 seconds;

2

- Crush slightly if recipe requires (this releases its flavour).

3

- Coarsely powder in a mortar and pestal, if recipe requires.

2

- Sauté vermicelli on low heat, stirring constantly, until light golden brown.

COOKING WITH TOMATOES

Deseeding tomatoes

I

- Cut tomato into quarters vertically, remove the seeds with a sharp knife.

2

- Cut as required in the recipe.

Roasting tomatoes

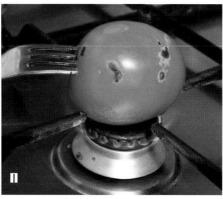

II

- Hold the head of the tomato with a fork over direct heat, turning all over, till the skin shrinks.

2

- Cool and remove the skin.

Grating tomatoes

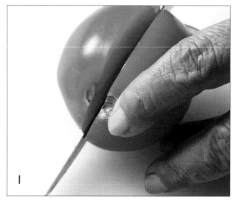

I

- Cut tomato into half, vertically.

2

- Grate from the cut side down till the tomato skin.

TOMATO GRAVY / TOMATO YOGHURT GRAVY

TIP
- The quantity of ingredients to be used as per recipe.

II

- Heat the oil in a pan; add asafoetida, cumin seeds.

2

- Add turmeric powder and red chilli powder; mix.

Making liquidized tomato

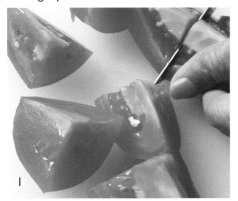

- Cut tomato into 8 pieces

- Blend in a food processor to a smooth paste.

ONION-TOMATO GRAVY

- Heat the oil; add bay leaves, cinnamon, cloves.

- Add grated onion, and ginger-garlic paste; fry till golden brown.

- Add red chilli powder and turmeric powder; mix.

- Add liquidized tomato and fry till oil separates.

- Add liquidized tomato, ginger, chilli paste. Cook till oil separates.

- To make tomato-yoghurt gravy, add beaten yoghurt to the cooked tomato gravy.

- Cook till oil separates. Add water.

WORKING WITH COTTAGE CHEESE

Making Plain Cottage Cheese *(paneer)*

- Bring 5 cups milk to the boil in a pan, on medium-heat, turn off heat. Add 1-2 tbsp lemon juice, gradually, stir till milk curdles.

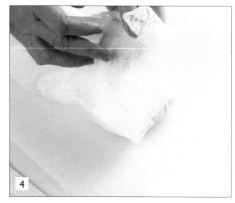

- Fold cloth over cottage cheese, moulding into a square shape.

- Wait for 2 minutes.

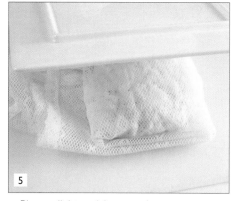

- Place a light weight over the cottage cheese for 20 minutes. Alternatively, place in a cottage cheese maker and cover with the lid for 20 minutes.

- Drain in a muslin cloth.

- Cut off any uneven edges. Use immediately or refrigerate for later use.

COTTAGE CHEESE TIP
- 5 cups milk makes 125 gm of cottage cheese.

Making Masala Cottage Cheese

- Boil 5 cups milk as above, add ¼ tsp salt, 1 tsp cumin seeds, 1 tsp chopped green chillies, and 2 tbsp coriander leaves, turn off the heat. Add 1-2 tbsp lemon juice, gradually, stir till milk curdles.

- Wait for 2 minutes. Drain.

- Place in a cottage cheese maker and cover with the lid for 20 minutes.

- Cut off any uneven edges. Use immediately or refrigerate for later use.

Sautéing Cottage Cheese

- Heat 2 tsp oil in a non-stick pan for 30 seconds; add cottage cheese and sauté on both sides, on medium heat, till light golden brown.

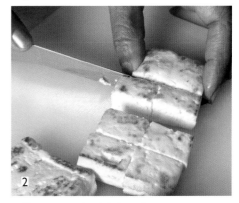

- Remove and cut into cubes.

BOILING RICE   MAKING DOUGH

1

- Wash and soak 1 cup rice in 4 cups water for 30 minutes. Drain.

1

- Sieve flour. Add all the ingredients (such as oil, clarified butter, yoghurt, milk) given in the recipe except water.

2

- Boil 6½ cups water. Add soaked rice, bring to the boil and cook, covered, on low heat till the rice is soft.

2

- Dough maybe soft, normal or hard. Adjust the quantity of water for a soft or hard dough, as required in the recipe.

3

- Remove, drain in a colander and transfer to a serving dish.

3

- Picture shows normal dough.

RICE TIP

- To check if the rice is cooked press with the index finger for softness.

DOUGH TIP

- Dough can be kneaded with hand or in a food processor.
- For normal dough, add 1½ cups water for 4 cups flour and knead well.

MAKING FRESH COOKING PASTES

Ginger Paste

1

- Take 2 tsp of chopped ginger.

2

- Hand pound chopped ginger to a fine paste, keep aside. Use as required.

3

Garlic Paste

1

- Take 8 garlic cloves.

2

- Hand pound chopped garlic cloves to a fine paste, keep aside. Use as required.

3

Chilli Paste

1

- Take 2 tsp of chopped green chillies.

2

- Hand pound chopped green chillies to a fine paste, keep aside. Use as required.

3

PRESSURE COOKING LENTILS / PULSES

Pressure cooking yellow lentil (*arhar dal*)

- Soak 125 gm lentil in 3 cups water for 30 minutes; drain. Put in a pressure cooker.

- Add 1½ cups water.

- Add ¾ tsp salt and ½ tsp turmeric powder. Pressure cook to one whistle and simmer for 4 minutes.
- Open the lid when the pressure drops.

Pressure cooking horse gram (*kala chana*)

- Soak 125 gm horse gram in 5 cups water for 8 hours; drain. Put in a pressure cooker.

- Pressure cook with 1¼ cups water and ¼ tsp salt to one whistle, simmer for 20 minutes. Open the lid when the pressure drops.

LENTIL TIP
- Make sure that the pressure drops before removing the lid to ensure that the lentils / pulses are fully cooked.

Pressure cooking chickpeas (*kabuli chana*)

- Soak 1 cup chickpeas in 5 cups water for 8 hours; drain. Put in a pressure cooker.

- Add 2½ cups water.

- Add ¼ tsp salt and cook to one whistle; simmer for 30 minutes. Open the lid when the pressure drops.

Pressure cooking kidney beans (*rajmah*)

- Soak ¾ cup beans in 4 cups water for 4 hours; drain.

- Put the beans in a pressure cooker and add 2 cups water.

- Add ¼ tsp turmeric powder and ¼ tsp salt; cook to one whistle and simmer for 30 minutes. Open the lid when the pressure drops.

Pressure cooking black eyed beans (*lobhia*)

- Soak ¾ cup beans in 4 cups water for 4 hours; drain. Put in a pressure cooker..

- Add 2 cups water.

- Add ¼ tsp turmeric powder and ¼ tsp salt; cook to one whistle and simmer for 5 minutes. Open the lid when the pressure drops.

TEMPERING LENTILS

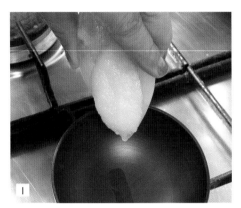

1

- Heat the clarified butter in a pan for 30 seconds.

2

- Add asafoetida.

Variation with curry leaves

1

- Heat the clarified butter in a pan for 30 seconds.

3

- Add cumin seeds and cook till the seeds start spluttering.

2

- Add mustard seeds and curry leaves.

4

- Remove from heat and add dry red chillies (if recipes requires) and red chilli powder or ground black pepper.

3

- Add red chilli powder.

COOKING WITH VEGETABLES

Blanching Beans and Carrots

- Boil 5 cups water, add 1 cup beans and carrots each.

- Blanch for 2 minutes.

- Drain in a colander.

Blanching of Bean Sprouts

- Boil 4 cups water and add 2 cups beans sprouts.

- Cook for 2 minutes, uncovered.

- Drain and use as per recipe.

TEMPERING TIP

- Removing the pan from the heat prevents chilli powder from getting burnt, as this will spoil the flavour of the dish.
- Follow quantity and ingredients in the order given in the recipe.

BLANCHING TIP

- Blanching, also called par-boiling, is lightly cooking raw vegetables for varying amounts of time in boiling water.

COOKING WITH VEGETABLES

• **Spinach**

• Heat the pan; add 500 gm chopped spinach and ¼ tsp sugar.

• **Fenugreek leaves**

• Cook covered for 2 minutes.

• Heat the pan; add 250 gm chopped fenugreek leaves and ¼ tsp sugar; cook covered for 1 minute.

• Remove and use as per recipe .

• Remove and use as per recipe.

Corn

- Heat 2 tsp oil in a pan for 30 seconds; add 2 cups corn and cook for 2 minutes, on high heat, stirring frequently.

- Peas

- Heat ½ tbsp oil in a pan; add 2 cups peas and ¼ tsp salt. Cook, covered, on low heat till soft.

- Remove and use as per recipe.

- Remove and use as per recipe.

TIP

- Adding ¼ tsp sugar while cooking spinach and fenugreek helps to retain the green colour.

WORKING WITH YOGHURT

- Setting yoghurt

- Heat 5 cups milk until lukewarm.

- **Making hung yoghurt for salad dressing:** place 2 cups yoghurt in a sieve or in a muslin cloth for 2-3 hours.

- Add ½ tsp yoghurt culture.

- **Making yoghurt for *raita* and *dahi pakodi*:** place 2 cups yoghurt (as per recipe) in a sieve for 30 minutes.

- Mix lukewarm milk and yoghurt culture thoroughly.

- Leave to set in a warm place for 3-6 hours. Refrigerate.

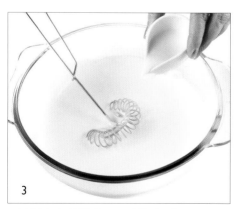

- Whisk. Add ¼-½ cup chilled milk to get a soft creamy consistency.

WHILE MAKING DESSERTS

- **Biscuit crumbs**

1

- Place 6 Marie biscuits in a bag.

- **Bread squeezing:**

1

- Dip 2-4 slices of bread in 2½ cups water.

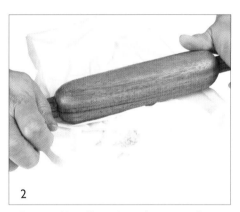

2

- Press with rolling pin to form crumbs.

YOGHURT TIP

- Always set yoghurt using lukewarm milk (40°-45°C). Putting culture into hot milk spoils the texture and taste of yoghurt.
- Yoghurt sets faster in summer while it takes longer in winter.
- Once set, refrigerate to prevent it from getting sour.

HUNG YOGHURT TIP

- Milk is normally added to get the right consistency and flavour.
- Hung yoghurt removes excess water and milk gives it a fresh taste.

3

- Add 2 tsp melted butter, mix. Place and press in a serving dish. Refrigerate for 45 minutes until firm. Follow the recipe.

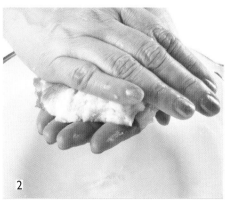

2

- Remove immediately and squeeze with your palms.

Whipped Cream

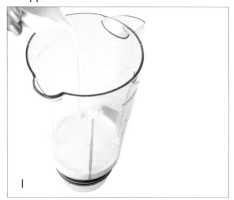

- Mix 1¼ Mcups chilled cream with ¼ cup chilled milk.

- Add 2 tbsp powdered sugar and 2 tsp rose water. Blend in a food processor till semi-thick.

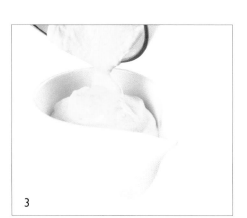

- Use as required in the recipe and consume within 24 hours.

Sugar Syrup

- Mix ¾ cup sugar with ¼ cup water in a shallow pan and bring to the boil, on low heat, stirring occasionally.

- To check the string, place a drop of syrup on a plate.

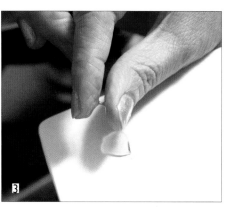

- Check between thumb and index finger.

CREAM MAKING TIPS
- Use chilled cream and milk to avoid curdling.
- Over blending may also lead to separation of butter from cream-milk mixture.
- For variation, use ½ tsp vanilla essence instead of rose water.

CUSTARD MAKING TIPS
- Custard powder should be mixed with room temperature milk otherwise it tends to get lumpy.

SUGAR SYRUP
- **One-string consistency**: a thin string is formed when testing the sugar syrup between thumb and index finger.
- **Two-string consistency**: when testing the sugar syrup between thumb and index finger, two strings are formed.

Custard

- Take 5 cups milk. Mix 4 tbsp custard powder in ½ cup milk.

- Boil the remaining 4½ cups milk with 4 tbsp sugar.

- Pour the custard mixture to the boiling milk, stirring constantly.

- Turn off the heat after one boil. Remove, keep aside to cool. Serve chilled

Jelly Making

- Mix 1 packet jelly crystals with 1 cup hot water.

- Add 1 cup cold water.

- Leave it to set in the fridge till firm. Remove with a knife / spoon. Serve chilled.

PEELING AND CHOPPING NUTS

1

- Soak ½ cup almonds in 1½ cups water for 8 hours, covered

1

- Soak ½ cup pistachios in 1½ cups water for 8 hours, covered.

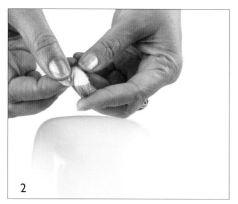

2

- Peel.

2

- Peel.

3

- Chop and refrigerate. Consume within 2 days.

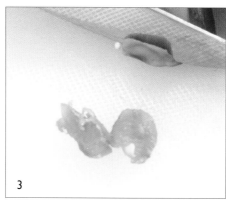

3

- Chop and refrigerate. Consume within 2 days.

TIP
- Peeled almonds and pistachios taste better in Indian desserts.

MAKING SAFFRON CARDAMOM POWDER

1

• Deseed 8 cardamom.

2

4

• Use quantities as indicated in each recipe.
• Saffron and cardamom can also be pounded individually.
• It can also be stored in the refrigerator for 15 days.

3

• Pound both to a fine powder.

MEAL MENUS

1

DRINK, SALAD & STARTER
Minty Lemonade
Hara Bhara Nimbu Pani   25
Salad Medley with Jaggery Dressing
Mila Jula Salaad   37
Cottage Cheese Fritters
Paneer Pakodi   44

MAIN COURSE
Lentil Dumplings and Spinach in Yoghurt Sauce
Magori Palak ki Kadi   77
Curried Kidney Beans
Rajmah   79
Potatoes and Capsicum
Aloo Shimla Mirch   82
Corn a la Cilantro
Dhaniyawale Makai ke Dane   96

RICE & BREADS
Cumin Pilaf
Jeera Pulao   124
Spicy Indian Bread
Masala Paratha   136
Plain Indian Bread
Sada Roti   137

ACCOMPANIMENT
Tempered Liquid Buttermilk
Tarka Mattha   152

DESSERT
Carrot Pudding
Gajar ka Halwa   173

2

DRINKS, SALADS & STARTER
Tomato Cucumber Melody
Tamatar Khira Lajawab   26
Tomato and Cottage Cheese Salad
Tamatar aur Masala Paneer Salaad   39
Sago Cutlets
Sabu Dana Vada   56

MAIN COURSE
Dumplings in Spicy Yoghurt Sauce
Kadi Pakodi   74
Fenugreek Flavoured Lentil
Urad Chana aur Methi Dal   80
Healthy Leafy Vegetables
Hara Saag   102
Mixed Vegetables with Cottage Cheese
Sabz Paneer   106

RICE & BREADS
Plain Rice
Crisp Indian Bread
Khasta Roti   139
Plain Indian Bread
Sada Roti   137

ACCOMPANIMENT
Plain Yoghurt

DESSERT
Fruit and Custard Pudding
Thanda Phalon ka Custard   169

3

DRINK, SALAD & STARTER
Iced Tea
Sharbati Chai   21
Corn Salad
Makai Salaad   34
Crispy Baby Corn
Chhote Karare Bhutte   43

MAIN COURSE
Roasted Spiced Eggplant
Baingan Bharta   90
Stuffed Green Chillies
Bharwa Mirchi   98
Curried Colocasia
Rasedar Arvi   110
Spicy Chickpeas
Chana Masala   112

RICE
Fenugreek Flavoured Cottage Cheese Pilaf
Methi Paneer Pulao   126

ACCOMPANIMENT
Spinach Flavoured Yoghurt
Palak Raita   153

DESSERT
Vermicelli Pudding
Sewai ki Kheer   171

4

DRINK, SALAD & STARTER

Tender Coconut Cooler
Daab Shikanji   24
Chickpea Salad
Kabuli Chana Salaad   33
Floret Fritters
Gobi Pakodi   45

MAIN COURSE

Spiced Green Bananas in Yoghurt Curry
Kele ki Kadi   73
Beans with Baby Corn
Beans aur Chhote Bhutte   94
Curried Lotus Stem
Sookhi Kamal Kakri   103
Cottage Cheese with Peas in Gravy
Mattar Paneer   117

BREAD

Flaky Mint Bread
Lachchedar Paratha   134
Plain Indian Bread
Sada Roti   137

ACCOMPANIMENT

Fruity Yoghurt
Anar aur Ananas Raita   147

DESSERT

Sunrise Pudding
Boondi Bake   168

5

DRINK, SALAD & STARTER

Spiced Yoghurt Drink
Mattha   20
Sweet Potato and Bean Sprout Salad
Chatpata Shakarkandi Salaad   38
Stuffed Chilli Fritters
Bharwa Mirchi ki Pakodi   47

MAIN COURSE

Stuffed Okra
Bharwa Bhindi   93
Hot Potato Curry
Aloo ka Jhol   108
Lentil Dumplings with Fenugreek and Peas
Methi Magori Mattar   118

RICE & BREAD

Mixed Vegetable Pilaf
Sabz Pulao   127
Carom Spiced Puffs
Namak Ajwain ki Puri   142

ACCOMPANIMENT

Lentil Dumplings in Creamy Yoghurt
Dahi Pakodi   149

DESSERT

Indian Rice Pudding
Chawal ki Kheer   170

6

DRINK, SALAD & STARTER

Mango Mocktail
Aam Panna   22
Potato and Pickled Onion Salad
Aloo Pyaz, Sirkewale   36
Potato Fritters
Aloo Pakodi   46

MAIN COURSE

Spicy Green Lentil
Sabut Moong ki Dal   81
Cauliflower and Potatoes
Aloo Gobi   88
Bottle Gourd Dumplings in Tomato Gravy
Lauki Kofta   114
Bitter Sweet Creamy Peas
Methi Malai Mattar   119

RICE & BREAD

Corn Pilaf
Bhutte ka Pulao   123
Plain Indian Bread
Sada Roti   137
Fenugreek Bread
Besan Methi Roti   138

ACCOMPANIMENT

Yoghurt with Lentil Pearls
Boondi Raita   148

DESSERT

Saffron Pistachio Delight
Kesar Pista Kulfi   175

COMMON ACCOMPANIMENTS

Green Chutney
Hari Chutney   154
Jaggery Flavoured Mango Chutney
Aam ki Launji   158

Lemon Flavoured Ginger
Nimbu ka Adrak   160
Tangy Radish Flakes
Mooli ka Kas   161

Green Chilli Pickle
Hari Mirch ka Achaar   162

SNACKS MENUS

1

Spicy Indian Puffs
Pani Puri   64
Spicy Chaat Bowls
Chaat Katori   66
Spicy Potato Patties
Chatpati Aloo Tikki   57
Lentil Dumplings in Creamy Yoghurt
Dahi Pakodi   149
Green Chutney
Hari Chutney   154
Sweet Chutney
Meethi Chutney   157

2

Lentil Pancakes
Moong Dal Cheela   51
Savoury Rice Flakes
Poha   60
Sago Cutlets
Sabu Dana Vada   56
Mushroom Cheese Toast
Khumbi Toast   54
Green Chutney
Hari Chutney   154
Sweet Chutney
Meethi Chutney   157

3

Toasted Garden Sandwiches
Hara Bhara Toast   55
Potato Fritters
Aloo Pakodi   46
Spicy Semolina
Rawa Upma   62
Dry green Lentil
Sookhi Moong Dal   50
Green Chutney
Hari Chutney   154
Sweet Chutney
Meethi Chutney   157

4

Vegetable Vermicelli
Sabzdar Sewai   63
Savoury Lentil Cakes
Chatpata Dhokla   52
Corn on Toast
Karare Makai Pav   42
Savoury Semolina Cakes
Rawa Idli   61
Coconut Chutney
Nariyal ki Chutney   156
Green Chutney
Hari Chutney   154

GLOSSARY OF FOOD AND COOKING TERMS

Bake	To cook in the oven by dry heat.	**Sauté**	To cook in an open pan in hot, shallow fat, tossing the food to prevent it from sticking.
Batter	A mixture of flour, liquid, and sometimes other ingredients of a thin, creamy consistency.	**Seasoning**	Salt, pepper, spices, herbs, and so forth, added to give depth of flavour.
Blend	To mix together thoroughly two or more ingredients.	**Shallow-fry**	A small quantity of fat is used, in a shallow pan. The food must be turned halfway through to cook both sides.
Coat	To cover food that is to be deep-fried with batter.		
Curdle	To separate milk into yoghurt and whey by acid or excessive heat.	**Simmer**	To boil gently on low heat.
Deep-fry	Sufficient fat is used to cover the food completely. The pan used must be deep enough to be only half full of fat before the food is added.	**Steam**	To cook food in steam. Generally food to be steamed is put in a perforated container which is placed above a pan of boiling water. The food should not come in contact with the water.
Fry	To cook in hot fat or oil.	**Stir-fry**	To fry rapidly while stirring and tossing.
Garnish	An edible decoration added to a dish to improve its appearance.	**Stock**	Liquid produced when vegetables are simmered in water with herbs and spices for several hours.
Grease	To coat the surface of a dish or tin with fat to prevent food from sticking to it.	**Syrup**	A concentrated solution of sugar in water.
Grind	To reduce hard food such as pulses, lentils, spices, and so forth, to a fine or coarse paste in a grinder or blender.	**Temper**	To fry spices and flavourings in hot oil or clarified butter, and to pour this over the main preparation.
Knead	To work a dough by hand or machine until smooth.	**Whisk**	To beat rapidly and introduce air into a light mixture; such as yoghurt.
Purée	To press food through a fine sieve or blend it in a blender or food processor to a smooth, thick mixture.		